82/1992

Meeting Needs
THROUGH
Support
Groups

Meeting Needs

THROUGH

Support Groups

How to Sponsor a Support Group
and Meet the Needs of . . .

Adult Children of Alcoholics
Divorced Persons
Single Parents
Chemically Dependent Persons
Bereaved Persons
Persons with AIDS
and many others.

SARA HINES MARTIN

Published by:
New Hope
P.O. Box 12065
Birmingham, Alabama 35202-2065

Bible verses taken from:
King James Version
Excerpts from New American Standard: Copyright 1960, 1962, 1963, 1968, 1971, 1972, 1973, 1975, 1977 by The Lockman Foundation. A Corporation Not for Profit, La Habra, California. All rights reserved. Printed in the United States of America. Used by permission.

Dewey Decimal Classification: 302.3
Subject Headings: GROUP RELATIONS TRAINING
                  SUPPORT GROUPS
                  HUMAN RELATIONS

Cover design by Barry Graham.

N923112•5M•0692
ISBN 1-56309-053-8

Meeting Needs Through Support Groups is a cooperative effort of Woman's Missionary Union, SBC, and Family Ministry Department of the Baptist Sunday School Board.

Contents

"Brethren, even if a man is caught in any trespass, you who are spiritual, restore such a one in a spirit of gentleness; each one looking to yourself, lest you too be tempted. Bear ye one another's burdens, and thus fulfill the law of Christ" (Gal. 6:1-2 NASB).

Prayer for Serenity
God, grant me the serenity
to accept the things I cannot change,
the courage to change the things I can,
and the wisdom to know the difference.
Living one day at a time,
enjoying one moment at a time;
accepting hardship as a pathway to peace;
taking, as Jesus did,
this sinful world as it is,
not as I would have it;
trusting that You will make all things right
if I surrender to Your will;
so that I may be reasonably happy in this life
and supremely happy with You forever in the next.
Amen.

Reinhold Niebuhr

Introduction

Support groups are everywhere. You can find them meeting in schools, community centers, hospitals, churches, and even places of work. You can even find them in the comics. In one strip I read, the character Shoe, sitting before his perpetually overflowing desk, says, "I feel a lot more secure in my messiness ever since I joined Messy Persons Anonymous, and they lent me their support."[1]

In another comic strip called "Alex's," a young man says to a coworker, "It says here there's a '12 Step' Support Group now for people who TALK TOO MUCH! It's called 'And On and On and On Anon.'"[2] (I would qualify to join that one!)

In a more serious vein, this letter appeared in Ann Landers' column:

Dear Ann,
For years, I couldn't go to a sports event, grocery store, restaurant, or movie for fear I'd have an anxiety attack. It was nearly impossible for me to work.
I became addicted to tranquilizers. Nothing worked. What turned my life around was meditating, going to support group meetings and reading books on anxiety and phobias.
A certain magic takes over when people who share the same problem get together to help each other.
Feeling Fit in Indiana

Ann responded:

> Dear Indiana,
>   I've been swamped with letters from people who have con-
> quered panic attacks. It is important to remember that a physi-
> cal exam to rule out a medical problem is essential. *Most read-
> ers, however, say they've had the greatest success with support
> groups and self-help books* (italics added).[3]

Groups have made a tremendous contribution to my life. I
have participated in therapy groups and in 12-step groups, support
groups which follow a 12-step format (see p. 28 for more information on 12-step groups). I echo the statement of the person from
Indiana. Support groups can be the key to turning a person's life
around. Groups sharing a common concern can enable healing to
begin for participants who work at it while attending the group.

I have also had experience in leading support groups. For two
years I served as a volunteer leader for a Parents' Anonymous
Group (now merged with the Georgia Council on Child Abuse).
It started as a support system for physically abusive parents, but
developed into a meeting for parents who needed help in dealing
with their children in general. That particular chapter met in a
Baptist church which donated meeting space and provided a volunteer nursery for parents. Leading that group was an especially
gratifying experience for me.

For a few months I led a support group for women incarcerat-
ed in a county jail. Most of the women had committed nonvio-
lent offenses, such as writing bad checks. One day, however, when
I asked the usual question, "Will each of you tell what brought
you here?" the woman to my left—close enough to touch—said,
"I've been convicted of murdering my husband."

I then recognized her from a newspaper photograph. It was a
highly publicized case in which the woman and her boyfriend had
shot her husband. That was an interesting moment for me; I had
never been that close to a murderer. She was transferred to the
state prison, however, and I never saw her again.

Leading that support group was also gratifying; unfortunately,
it came to an end when the jail was closed to volunteer work. I'm
ready to go back whenever the door opens.

Although I did not lead a support group for rape survivors, I underwent training for it at the Rape Crisis Center at Grady Memorial Hospital in Atlanta and served as a volunteer to rape survivors.

In researching this book, I visited churches; interviewed pastors, other staff members, and laypersons; and saw the 'footprints of Jesus' wher'er I went. Much healing is taking place within support group meetings. Churches are being the hands of Jesus as they work with group members. In this book you will find true accounts of persons involved in a variety of support groups. Most names have been changed to protect persons, although a few asked that I specifically use their names. Their stories show how God is bringing about healing in the context of small groups of persons who face similar problems.

Also, in this book, you will find guidelines for sponsoring and/or developing support groups within your church. Some guidelines are woven in chapter material (especially guidelines related to the chapter's particular issue); general guidelines are identified in the chapter "Foundations." Although you may be tempted to skip chapters which deal with issues you are not addressing, I suggest you don't. You may discover valuable information in those chapters which would be of help to you.

It is my prayer that the healing that others and I have experienced through groups may come to many others through your dedicated, caring leadership.

Sara Hines Martin

[1]"Shoe." Reprinted by permission: Tribune Media Services.
[2]"Alex's." Reprinted with special permission of King Features Syndicate, Inc.
[3]Permission granted by Ann Landers and Creators Syndicate.

Foundations

What Is a Support Group?

Church growth leaders agree that small groups are an effective way to reach people and meet needs. The group process has proved to be the most effective method for helping persons addicted to alcohol and other drugs, and to help codependents stop the enabling behaviors inherent in codependent behavior.

Exactly what is a support group?

In its simplest definition, a support group is a peer-led group of individuals who share a common need and who meet on a regular basis in a confidential setting. They share what is happening in their lives, receive encouragement from each other, and learn and grow in the process. They speak for themselves rather than give advice to others.

Confidentiality and refraining from advice-giving are the hallmarks of a support group. In a healthy support group, members feel free to be themselves, warts and all.

This style of support group has enormous potential for helping individuals who might never meet with a professional mental health worker.

According to Bill Porter, a Christian therapist in Atlanta, Georgia, "Some Christians fear the term self-help group because they think it suggests that we do not rely on God's help; but self-help refers to the fact that no professional therapist works with the group and that the group charges nothing."

The Rapha Right Step Christian Recovery Program identifies three basic types of support groups: therapy groups, self-help groups, and Christ-centered groups. They have developed a program to train Christians to facilitate Christ-centered 12-step programs for chemical dependents and codependents in churches. According to their guidebook for this program, "[Christ-centered groups] do not exist to provide therapy and are not limited just to individuals sharing with one another. The Right Step Groups offer individuals a time of sharing and education. Our spiritual direction and unity are based on the Word of God and the acknowledgment of Jesus Christ as Lord and Savior."[1]

In this book, I use the term *self-help groups* to refer to groups where peers lead the interaction. Some support groups follow a 12-step format; others have sharing only; some combine study and sharing; some have sharing and study within a 12-step format.

Roots of Groups in the Christian Experience

In his doctoral project on support groups for pastors, David Platt, a pastor in Sudbury, Massachusetts, states that a general survey of the Bible reveals the story of God acting through the lives of persons. More specifically, God works through groups of people, such as families, communities, or entire nations.

Christianity began with a small group of people—Jesus "appointed twelve, that they might be with Him" (Mark 3:14 NASB). Jesus called them friends, not servants. They were bound together in communion with God and with one another.

A small group gathered in the upper room after Jesus' crucifixion. Those men were distressed, defeated, discouraged, scared, and lonely. They had just lost the person who meant the most to them in all the world. They probably chose this room because it was, more than likely, the room where they had eaten the Last Supper with their Lord.

What did these people do in the upper room? They talked, shared, and comforted one another and bonded in a unique way. It was there that the promise of the Holy Spirit's ministry (see John 14-17) became a reality. Henri Nouwen, author of *The Wounded Healer*, says, "The 'walking wounded' became the 'wounded healers' and went out to accomplish the things that are recorded in the book of Acts."

Charles Shirley, a chaplain and retired missionary, wrote in his doctoral project on small group ministry in the church:

> There is some deep resistance to the idea on the part of both religious leaders and church members to the idea of small group ministry in the church. Types and approaches have greatly proliferated which have produced confusion. The term 'small group' has many connotations, some of them negative. I have the impression that the fear is that a small group might either be conducted with inept leadership with the possibility of some disagreeable results or might produce experiences which would be out of keeping with the other aspects of church life.
>
> There is some foundation to these fears. One of the principles of responsible group work is that the approach must harmonize with the institutional setting. A therapy-type model does not harmonize with the environmental mood or tone of most congregations. Furthermore, groups majoring on deep emotional expressions require well-trained leaders.[2]

"The church today faces many problems," Shirley concludes. "No one approach will solve all of these. Small groups—with their vitality and fellowship—are appropriate and effective in revitalization efforts, but these are only aspects of the total church ministry. If this perspective is maintained, a small group ministry will not be burdened with too many expectations and much good will be accomplished."[3]

Platt says, "My theology is undeniably incarnational. That is, one of the most important ways God comes to His children is through other people. After all, it is in the person of Jesus Christ that God has come to His world most fully. And God's call is to community with an encouragement to 'bear one another's burdens, and so fulfill the law of Christ' (see Gal. 6:2 NASB). There, each follower of Christ is urged to be a channel of God's support and grace to others,"[4] Platt concludes.

Platt comments, "The fact that support groups are needed is a reflection of the kind of society in which we live. Under the cultural pressure to succeed (and to do so by competition), deep friendships are discouraged rather than encouraged. To stem this tide, an alternative force is needed. To organize a group for spiritual and personal support is one avenue. To belong to a community is to meet with other fellow strugglers in 'life together.' The healing power of community is a resource sorely needed by . . . servants of God. Life experienced in koinonia is the key to their transformation."[5]

Value of Groups

Literally tens of thousands of people each year participate in small groups. Why have groups become so popular in our society?

American society, which is increasingly technological and dehumanizing, leaves people feeling empty. When they come together in a group, they can talk about their concerns and problems for the purpose of learning new ways of thinking, feeling, doing, or being which will make their lives better.

Too often in today's world, people treat others in impersonal ways which show indifference to them as persons. They are not moved by the sufferings of others, and they behave cruelly, brutally, and in an unkind manner.

Many conditions in society act to dehumanize us: bureaucratic organizations; the increasing use of machines; and the mobility of people (which leads to short-term relationships), among others. One 1,600 member church which considered itself traditional with a settled membership found that only five percent of the families had been members for more than five years. This is the norm in our nation now, not the exception. Extended family situations, which used to be a mechanism for help and support to members, rarely exists anymore. The average American family now moves every five years.

In contrast, Christian relationship is characterized by kindness, mercy, consideration, tenderness, love, concern, compassion, responsiveness, and friendship. God created us with the need for relationships—with Him as well as with others (see Eccl.

4:9-10; Phil. 4:19). Jesus Christ gave us the example to follow in His relationships with others. His encounters with the woman at the well in John 4, the man with the paralyzed hand in Matthew 6, and the story of the prodigal son in Luke 15 all exhibit deep concern for the whole person. He responded to their needs—seen and unseen—and treated them with respect and compassion. In Matthew 25:31-46, He gave Christians the mandate to follow suit.

Support groups allow people to expand their relationships and receive support and encouragement. As a professional counselor, I often act as a "paid friend" for a client. I think this role could just as well be performed by a support group.

Individuals who praise the use of support groups are likely to be those who have experienced such groups. Critics are likely to be those who have had no such personal experience.

[1] *Rapha Right Step Christian Recovery Program Facilitator Training Manual.* (Houston, Rapha Publishing, 1990), p. IV-2.

[2] Charles Shirley. "The Religious Discussion-Interaction Group: An Experience in Small Group Ministry." (Dmin. diss., Southeastern Baptist Theological Seminary, 1973).

[3] Ibid.

[4] David Platt. "A Program of Spiritual Group Support for Pastors in the Greater Boston Baptist Association." (Dmin. diss., Southern Baptist Theological Seminary, 1989).

[5] Ibid.

Guidelines for Leaders of Support Groups and Growth Groups

So the idea of helping people appeals to you. . . .

So you have participated, perhaps, in either a therapy group, a support group, and/or a 12-step group. . . .

So you know your community has a great need for the kind of help that support groups offer. . . .

So you take Christ's commands about ministering to others in His name seriously. . . .

So you've identified the ability to lead as one of your spiritual gifts. . . .

What do you do to get a support group started in your church?

Discover the Need

Research the needs in your area and identify which ones are going unmet. Find out what kinds of support groups are already meeting locally. Look for unmet needs instead of duplicating existing ministries. Your pastor, minister of education, and other church staff members may be able to identify needs. Also, talk with local social service agencies, social workers, and hospitals to discover existing support groups and the need for other groups. Survey existing conditions in your community. For example, a high jobless rate could indicate a need for a support group for unemployed persons.

Enlist Support

Present your proposal for a support group to the appropriate approving body in the church, such as the church council. Every church is different, so follow the procedures for yours. If you are part of a church organization which seeks to sponsor the support group, follow the procedures set out for that group.

Publicize the Group

Publicize the group inside and outside the church. Inside the church, utilize available avenues of publicity, such as church newsletter, Sunday School class announcements, and worship service announcements.

Outside the church, publicize in a variety of ways. Consider public service announcements in a local newspaper or on a local television station or a cable television bulletin board. Support group listings often appear in the health or life-style section of newspapers.

Notify persons in your area who are in positions to refer others to a growth group or support group. Consider these persons: social workers; doctors; psychiatrists, psychologists, and other counselors; law enforcement officers; hospital community relations workers; schools; other churches; crisis center workers.

Tailor publicity to your group's topic, as much as possible. For example, notify local employment agencies of a support group for unemployed persons. Consider running an announcement for it in the classified section of the newspaper. Place publicity for groups in places where persons who need such a group will see it. Use creativity and sensitivity in creating publicity.

Prepare Yourself

A person who leads a support group is usually called a facilitator, not leader. A facilitator of a support group should possess the following characteristics:

1. Spiritual: The facilitator should love the Lord, have a consistent prayer life, be a growing Christian, and be known in the church as a stable, mature Christian. Leading a group must come from the Lord's leadership rather than from ego needs of one's own. The facilitator must recognize that while people are sinners, God can help them change.

2. Social: The facilitator should love people, enjoy being around others, and be caring and nonjudgmental. The facilitator should be a good listener and possess the ability to create a warm atmosphere within a group. The facilitator should be able to draw quiet members out.

The facilitator must detach from the group process—not claim credit for successes, nor blame for failures.

The facilitator must recognize and value the contributions of others.

The facilitator must not be a controller. A controlling leader will kill a group.

3. Emotional: The facilitator must have worked through any personal issues to a significant degree and possess emotional stability. He or she should be aware of one's personal feelings—positive and negative. One's actions and words must match. People must view him or her as "real." He or she must possess a high level of Christian self esteem. The facilitator must be realistic about one's own capabilities. The facilitator must model personal openness before the group.

The facilitator must be trustworthy. He or she must be capable of treating confidential information as just that—confidential.

A facilitator must not avoid criticism to the extent that it undermines efforts. He or she must be able to handle anger and rejection. Group members may express anger at times. The anger may be displaced, but it can hurt.

The facilitator should have a support system where he or she can process his or her own frustrations, hurts, etc.

4. Personal: A facilitator must be fairly well organized and must enjoy learning. He or she must be disciplined enough to stick to a task but without being a workaholic. It may be tempting to quit when problems arise. The facilitator must possess effective communication skills and skills for handling conflict.

The facilitator must desire to learn and continue improving group-leading skills.

Finally, the facilitator must cooperate with others in the church and not make the group a personal crusade.

All persons I interviewed who work with support groups within their churches spoke in one accord: The person who plans to lead a crisis-oriented support group in a church (groups which deal with highly stressful life situations) must attend a 12-step recovery program to work through his or her own recovery program. A person cannot learn to lead such a group simply by reading material.

For the facilitator of a crisis-oriented group, it would be helpful to attend open meetings of Alcoholics Anonymous and other similar groups, such as Al-Anon.

Go with an open mind and without a judgmental attitude. AA and Al-Anon are not church. Individuals who attend them come from all walks of life, and the primary aim of AA is to get people sober!

Dr. Edwin Lilly, national missionary for the Southern Baptist Home Mission Board and former director of the Clovis A. Brantley Baptist Center, says, "In working with street people, I've been cursed out in several languages. Don't let language become a barrier to helping people."

If you prefer, attend a group which is sponsored by another church. Attend at least six times before drawing a conclusion about the group.

Basic Guidelines for Groups

A group needs structure to give it boundaries. Structure gives members security and calls on them to be accountable. In 12-step support groups, the format is adhered to strictly. If a member breaks a rule, the facilitator speaks to him in a courteous manner. Support groups which do not follow a given format should agree at the beginning on basic rules group members will observe. These objectives may be read at the beginning of each meeting.

The main rules in support groups relate to confidentiality and cross talking.

Support groups **must** maintain confidentiality, especially in crisis-oriented groups. Persons who attend must know that what they say will not be repeated outside the meeting. Lack of confidentiality inhibits group trust. Without trust the group is ineffective.

Groups must also avoid cross talk. Cross talk is arguing with or verbally attacking another member, giving advice, responding with criticism, verbally responding to every statement made, or confronting in any way. The facilitator must have the authority to speak up when someone cross talks. The speaker may get hurt feelings and never return, but if that rule is not observed, the group itself could collapse. The facilitator needs to speak privately with the offender after the meeting to assure that the action was not meant personally. A leader should tactfully interrupt a speaker who dominates discussion. A person who breaks confidentiality may be asked to leave. Some groups devise a written contract for members.

Members must be free to talk or not to talk. Some groups systematically give each person the opportunity to talk. A person who does not wish to talk may say, "I pass."

Facilitators must not process their own issues at the expense of the group. They do participate, but a balance must be maintained. One church support group collapsed because the husband/wife co-facilitators processed their own marital issues in the group.

The format must be followed even if only a few persons attend. It may be tempting to relax the boundaries and chitchat, but discipline is important. People sometimes say things within the safety of a structured setting that they won't say elsewhere.

Facilitators and members need to be comfortable with silence. During those lulls, timid persons sometimes gain the courage to speak and talkative members start speaking more thoughtfully. The facilitator must not "rescue" the meeting and try to make things happen when silence occurs. The group interaction belongs to the members, and the meeting needs to move at the pace dictated by the needs of those present.

If prolonged silences become the norm, the facilitator can ask what the silence is about. If individuals are clamming up because of angry feelings, they need to talk about it. The group may request to view a film or have a guest speaker at times.

The group's schedule needs to be followed. If people learn that the closing time will be extended to accommodate persons who still want to speak, they may delay speaking. When they know that the meeting will close on time, they are encouraged to use the time efficiently.

Some persons may feel frustrated by not getting to speak, but meetings do not need to guarantee that people will never experience any frustration. Learning to deal with frustration and delayed gratification is a maturing process. Individuals who do not have time to speak may become more assertive about speaking up quicker in future meetings. If a group becomes so large that members do not have adequate time to speak and/or people feel intimidated, a new group needs to be started.

People who cause problems need to be viewed as people with problems, not problem people. An excessive talker needs to be restrained. During a pause, the facilitator can say, "Thank you. Let's move on." If the behavior continues, the facilitator needs to speak to the person after the meeting, reminding him or her to keep comments within a reasonable time frame.

A romance which develops between participants may interfere with the group. Persons recovering from an addiction and/or codependency are encouraged to refrain from romantic involvements during the first year of recovery.

Accountability, which calls upon persons to be responsible to keep commitments, is a cornerstone of support groups. Group members must keep the rules of the group, such as confidentiality and no cross talk. An effective group must have a group member or members who have the power to set limits and who call upon other members to stay within or return to within the limits. Accountability also helps keep the group on track.

Confrontation takes place within therapy groups but not 12-step groups and support groups. Confrontation should be done through "I" statements to another member, such as, "I'm feeling angry," not "You make me angry."

If a psychologically ill person attends, the facilitator needs to privately encourage that person to seek professional help. The leader may also need to set limits on how long that person speaks. A facilitator needs to recognize when he or she needs help handling a person with a problem, when someone needs therapeutic help beyond what the group can offer, or when a member speaks of suicide.

A facilitator needs to recognize personal burnout and take a break, if necessary.

Children must not come to meetings.

Additional guidelines for leading support groups are given through the examples used in this book.

Kinds of Groups

Growth Groups

"The small group approach is a natural in the church, undergirded by a long tradition," Howard Clinebell says in the book, *Growth Groups*. "The right of each person to develop his full potential as a child of God is basic in the Jewish-Christian heritage. Many church leaders—clergy and laity—are discovering the power of groups for implementing this right . . . In the small, sharing group," Clinebell maintains, "lies the power which enables persons to love more fully and live more creatively."

Clinebell points out that churches which want to be relevant in our society have a three-pronged mission: to heal brokenness, nurture growth, and equip persons to help others and to create a more caring society. Growth groups are useful in each of these thrusts.

George Webber states his conviction that a congregation "will make basic provisions for its members to meet in small groups (as well as corporate worship), not as a sidelight or option for those who like it, but as a normative part of its life."[1]

Clinebell points out that an institution is vital to the extent that it is meeting human needs. People experience love, reconciliation, and grace in small communities of caring.

To continue growing, every person requires a depth relationship with at least one other human being. A small network of depth relationships is even better. The group is an interpersonal laboratory for testing and learning better ways of relating to others. It provides a place to do one's 'growth work'—the struggle to let go of costly but comfortable defenses which keep persons from growing.

Groups seem to be the most effective means for the most people to experience coming alive within themselves and in their relationships with other people. People who already function on a high level can break out of their boxes; they can uncover hidden strengths; and they can put depth into their intimate relationships.

In small towns where everyone knows everyone else, people usually fear sharing personal information and insights. The best type of group to have in this setting is one in which personal sharing is combined with structured study. Growth groups have three characteristics (adapted from Clinebell):

1. A primary (though not only) purpose is to help each member grow emotionally, interpersonally, intellectually, and spiritually.
2. A leadership style that brings about growth is used—first by the leader which, over a period of time, enables everyone to grow.
3. The goal focuses on discovering latent potential in each member, enabling them to be more effective in current living, and leading them to set positive goals for the future rather than looking backward at failures, problems, and sickness.[2]

To be most effective, a growth group needs to have these other characteristics:

4. The group is made up of highly functional people, and the goal is to make well people better. In therapy groups, led by professional counselors, sickness is the emphasis; in growth groups, health is the emphasis.
5. The group size is small enough so that members can develop trust and develop deep relationships.
6. Members blend personal feelings with the content, i.e., members learn while sharing feelings.

Growth groups often use study or discussion on a certain topic. Members deal with the content on a personal level, in terms of their feelings, struggles, hopes, and goals.

Clinebell believes that a good growth group aims at a balanced emphasis on the three interdependent dimensions of human development: inreach, outreach, and upreach.

In summary, he says, "a growth group provides an interpersonal environment in which persons can become more aware, relating, authentic, loving, enjoying, spontaneous, creating, risking, present, coping, and connected with [God]."[3]

Examples of Growth Groups

Examples of growth groups include:

- marriage preparation groups,
- marriage enrichment groups,
- singles groups,
- dialogue groups between parents and youth,
- groups to cope with stress,
- bereavement groups.

Key factors in creating an environment in which people grow include: Regular meetings (usually weekly), with a length of one-and-a-half to two hours; some type of marathon meeting occasionally (from three to six hours); an occasional all day meeting; an occasional retreat; and an intensive seminar or workshop.

An environment that provides growth must meet often enough, with a high level of intensity, and with sufficient ongoing group experience so that the group dynamics which govern how a group will operate can take place.

Groups which provide the greatest amount of growth for members decide upon a definite termination date—from 6 to 12 sessions. The optimal size is seven to twelve persons, in addition to the leader(s). If the goal is to learn information, the group can be larger than if the goal is for members to share.

Open groups admit members on an ongoing basis. Closed groups do not add members after the second meeting.

The meeting place needs to allow for privacy and comfort. A home does not provide an ideal setting due to possible interruptions.

Naming a Group

People face two fears regarding growth groups: they think that people who join such groups must have big problems, and they fear that if they get into such a group, they will be forced to share personal material they would rather keep private. The group name can help allay some fears.

The name of a growth group needs to be positive and nondramatic, such as: "Marriage Enrichment Group" or "Personal Growth Group."

Who Would Benefit from a Growth Group?

Any person who:
- has relationships within a functional range (not pathological);
- has a reasonable level of self esteem;
- wants to increase the quality of his relationships, increase his self-awareness, and/or use his talents more effectively;
- shares a common issue or concern with others and desires to explore that issue or concern.

What Happens in the First Meeting?

At a first meeting, members get acquainted and begin sharing with each other on a deeper level. They develop a "contract"—an agreement on what they plan to contribute and what they hope to gain from the experience.

The leader lays down guidelines to serve as boundaries for group interaction, such as:

1. Personal feelings and viewpoints are treated with respect.
2. Members talk about what they are struggling with in the present rather than spend time dealing with pain from the past. Sharing past events occurs only as it impacts the present.
3. All sharing is confidential. Nothing is repeated outside the group.
4. Members are encouraged to use what they learn in the sessions to improve the quality of their lives and relationships outside the group. Members share their own experiences rather than give advice.
5. Members agree to attend each session unless circumstances

prevent them from doing so.

6. Members agree to attend four to six sessions before deciding to leave, if they feel unhappiness in the beginning.

Stages in a Group

Stage one—anxiety. Members learn to connect with each other and to respect the leadership rather than try to take over.

Stage two—warmth. Members feel delighted to be in a place where it feels safe to share personal material openly without fear of rejection.

Stage three—frustration. Members may feel discouraged at the slowness of progress or they may resist going deeper.

Stage four—trust. Members exhibit caring, but they also confront one another.

Stage five—growth. Members experience breakthroughs in behavior.

Stage six—termination. Several sessions prior to ending, the leader reminds members of the closing date so that they can take care of work they want to do.

Closing Each Session

1. Tie up loose threads; allow members to make any statements they need to make before leaving.

2. Ask what they plan to do the coming week to further growth.

3. Allow participants to make statements as to how they felt about the session.

4. Have a closing ceremony such as a prayer, a song, a group hug, etc.

12-Step Support Groups

Twelve step programs began with Alcoholics Anonymous, but have since been adapted to more than 200 organizations which address other addictions. The steps were developed in 1935 by a group of recovering alcoholics.

What does it mean to work the steps? That means a person moves through each step, at his or her own pace, doing what each step requires. Working the steps has brought recovery and serenity to numbers of people. The steps are to be worked in order, but are never "completed." Working the steps takes considerable time and effort.

Christian groups have adapted the 12 steps for their use. The following listing of the 12 steps is adapted from the *Rapha Right Step Christian Recovery Program Facilitator Training Manual.*[4]

1. We admit that by ourselves we are powerless over our addiction and codependency—that our lives have become unmanageable.
2. We come to believe that God, through Jesus Christ, can restore us to sanity.
3. We make a decision to turn our lives over to God through Jesus Christ.
4. We make a searching and fearless moral inventory of ourselves.
5. We admit to God, ourselves, and to another human being the exact nature of our wrongs.
6. We commit ourselves to obedience to God, desiring that He remove patterns of sin from our lives.
7. We humbly ask God to renew our minds so that our sinful patterns can be transformed into patterns of righteousness.
8. We make a list of all persons we have harmed, and become willing to make amends to them all.
9. We make direct amends to such people where possible, except when doing so will injure them or others.
10. We continue to take personal inventory, and when we are wrong, promptly admit it.
11. We seek to grow in our relationship with Jesus Christ through prayer, meditation, and obedience, praying for wisdom and power to carry out His will.
12. Having had a spiritual awakening, we try to carry the message of Christ's grace and restoration power to others who are addicted or codependent, and to practice these principles in all of our affairs.

"I Lead a Christian 12-Step Program"

Diane, 43, belongs to a Baptist church in a suburb of a major city. Raised in an alcoholic family, she started drinking as a teenager.

Three abusive marriages, one child, three abortions, and two divorces later, a sister-in-law called her and said, "You must go with me to this church I've found. Jesus is there, there is so much love. It's a new church and I sing in the choir."

"One Sunday, I went," Diane says. "I was not raised in church and I didn't know what to do or how to talk 'church talk.' My sister-in-law was right about the love there."

Diane asked Jesus to forgive her of her sins and take control of her life. She was baptized.

She identified herself as a codependent and an alcoholic. Salvation took away Diane's desire for alcohol and drugs. "It was harder to give up smoking," she remembers.

Her third husband left her, and after hearing nothing for three years, Diane divorced him.

Diane's pastor approached her about attending classes sponsored by a Christian hospital for drug and alcohol dependency to learn to facilitate support groups. She now leads a group composed of recovering alcoholics and addicts and codependents.

"I felt very apprehensive," she says. "As a codependent, I want to control." Before Diane led her first meeting, she said to the Lord, "I'm going to show up; you use me. I can't do this." Her voice shook as she led, but she knew that her only job was to keep the group moving according to format.

The group conscience meeting (participants who volunteer to take care of the administration of the group), usually held once a month after a regular support group meeting, helps. Diane asks those who attend the group conscience meeting, "How do you feel about what's going on?" Participants in the support group started cross talking, so in the group conscience meeting, the members addressed the issue and agreed to work on the problem.

Diane tells support group participants, "Leave your masks at the door. Here, we're real." She sees members growing and changing, fighting battles and winning.

"My joy comes in seeing what the Lord is doing in my life and in others in the group. I see them opening up."

She observes, "Some of the healthiest persons in the church are those working a 12-step program."

[1]Clinebell, Howard. *Growth Groups*. (Nashville: Abingdon, 1978), p. 128.
[2]Ibid, p. 3.
[3]Ibid, pp. 6-7.
[4]*Rapha Right Step Christian Recovery Program Facilitator Training Manual*. (Houston, Rapha Publishing, 1990), p I-15. 12 Steps adapted and used by permission.

Family Issue-related Growth Groups and Support Groups

Support Groups for Families

Larry Matthews, pastor of Vienna Baptist Church, Vienna, Virginia, near Washington, DC, has started various support groups for families.

In 1976, he started a group for parents of teens because of difficulties teenage children were having in school. "I believe that parents who are given peer support do the best job," he says. "Two of those groups developed."

Seven years later, the church started a group for parents of children. Adults who responded were all parents of newborns. Two groups developed for that population.

For blended families and for individuals separating and divorcing, the church created a group called Families in Change.

The church provides a short-term Grief Support Group for the post-Christmas and post-Easter seasons.

A Crisis Support Group meets for anyone undergoing any type of stressful life situation: aging or ill parents, terminal illness, marital issues, etc.

Each fall, a kick-off meeting takes place for the church to present the groups to the congregation and visitors. The group facilitators describe the purposes of the groups.

Matthews keeps in touch with the facilitators on an ongoing basis. A Pastoral Counseling Center meets in the church building, and professionals provide supervision for facilitators. Some group members seek counseling at the center.

The Parents of Teens group sponsors two annual retreats

which are open to anyone. Pertinent topics, such as discipline, are discussed.

"Our requirement for persons to lead a group is that they must have participated as a member of some group for at least two years," Matthew says. "If persons exhibit change and growth in their lives, we consider them to serve as facilitators."

Support Group for Parents of Children with Rare Diseases

Susan Calhoun, (Mrs. Jim), lives in Conyers, Georgia, about 20 minutes from downtown Atlanta. Four of her five children are disabled. Her oldest daughter, Jennifer, died at age two-and-a half. Megan died in 1983 at 16 months. The couple has two sons, Matthew, 18, and Davis, 11.

The children have a rare disease called mitochondria. Little is known about it except that it is passed through the mother. The disease causes developmental delays and degenerative retinal problems, among other things. Its effects vary in girls and boys.

After Megan's death, Susan Calhoun could find no support system in metro-Atlanta for parents of children with a rare disease nor one for parents of children who didn't fall into a specified situation such as Down's Syndrome, spina bifida, or cystic fibrosis. She decided to start a support system for parents of children aged birth to adolescence with any handicap. The purposes of the group are to provide emotional support, provide information, and give physical support.

The support groups meet monthly or bimonthly in different locations around the seven-county metro-Atlanta area. Family activities take place three or four times a year, allowing interaction between parents, children, and siblings. Hospital visits are made to parents whose children have received critical diagnoses or who need support from parents in similar situations.

Each fall, the groups host an educational conference for professionals and parents to help with the coping process. The Fairy Godmother Program provides volunteers willing to stay with children in the hospital to relieve parents and/or to give love and friendship if the parents are not available.

A bereavement support group gives parents who have lost

children the opportunity to share their grief and feelings as well as to encourage and draw strength from one another. "I'm excited to see a support network coming about," Calhoun says. "I'd like to see churches get involved." She works with Ann Putnam of the Southern Baptist Convention's Home Mission Board, who is associate director of the Church and Community Ministries Department, working with the disabled in congregations.

Support Group for Infertile Couples

Doyle Hamilton, a pastoral counselor, wrote his doctoral project on infertile couples because of a personal interest—he and his wife, Salley, were both treated for infertility.

Infertility affects one out of every six marriages, including couples who have miscarriages and no births.

Since most churches are family oriented, Hamilton explains, childless couples can feel left out and hurt.

Hamilton led an eight-week support group for four infertile couples in a Baptist church. He found the couples were dealing with the following issues:

1. They ask, "Why me, Lord?" They feel confused, frustrated, defeated, and angry and resentful toward God; they feel like failures.
2. Some individuals may consider childlessness as God's judgment on them.
3. The couples feel "different," and feel a sense of isolation from the community.

"The main thing a couple needs to deal with is their grief," Hamilton says. "Infertility is basically a grief process, a loss of dreams, of hope, of expectations. The grief object, however, is intangible.

"The couples stated that the greatest benefit was to have an opportunity to talk about their 'private and personal pain,' a phrase they coined."

During the last meeting of his group, Hamilton announced that his wife, Salley, was pregnant. The group members rejoiced.

Churches need education about infertility, Hamilton maintains. Conducting a seminar would be helpful. Surveying the church and community would be a good way to alert the staff and congregation of the need for a ministry to this population. Infertile couples need to be acknowledged. A support group would be an extremely beneficial service. Hamilton considers eight weeks too short for a group. "An ongoing group would be best," he observes. "People need a long time to work through grief, accept infertility, and develop some options, such as adoption and/or childlessness."

It would be best if the group leader has dealt with the problem of infertility personally, but a sensitive person who becomes knowledgeable about the dynamics of infertility can do an effective job.

Families Victorious Support Group

Buck Clements and his wife, Mary, lead a support group called Families Victorious in the Martinez Baptist Church, Martinez, Georgia. The group was founded as the initial support group in a drug and alcohol program started by former associate pastor Roger Bennett.

When Bennett proposed starting a support group, Clements said, "That's a neat idea, but this is the wrong place. I don't think we will be able to carry this off in a conservative Southern Baptist church." He heard the same thought echoed throughout the congregation.

Bennett pressed the issue, and some church members were willing to try. "Then the Lord stepped in and things began to change, and we began to see the changes," Clements states.

"My wife and I are there because our son was involved in drug abuse and has been through a treatment center," Clements explains. In dealing with their son's drug problem, the couple felt "that we were the only deacon family who had a son involved in a drug-recovery program." What the Clementses discovered was that they were not the only ones—there were other people who were hurting, too. The church formed Families Victorious.

Families Victorious opens with prayer and words of encouragement. Quite often, they offer the opportunity for anyone who

35

is present and experiencing hurt to talk. "There's no point in dealing with Scripture or any other agenda if persons need to express themselves," Clements points out. The group follows a 12-step format and uses a 12-step workbook for group meetings. Often, members bring books and other available literature to meetings for the group to discuss. "Sometimes we look at selected Scripture," Clements explains. The group has built up a library of books available for check out. Clements also seeks out Christian counselors who are willing to donate their time to speak to the group occasionally.

Involvement in the group has brought joy to Buck and Mary Clements. "I have been leader of the group for more than two years. Had I been involved in any other program within the church, I probably would have experienced some burnout by now, but this particular program is a passion, it is not an obligation. I don't feel trapped into having to take this role. I have gained far more from the program than I have given," Clements says.

"I can see within our church that healing is underway. We're no longer feeding people with an "empty spoon," as I always felt. At one time we simply offered encouragement to people and we told them that we loved them; but now wherever they are, whether it's in the gutter or in the pews, we try to be with them, instead of behind them," Clements says.

Clements learned the concept of an "empty spoon" from a book written by a teacher in an underprivileged area. She discovered she could not teach the children because they came to school hungry. Their physical needs had to be met first. The teacher began to feed the children breakfast, and they began responding to her teaching.

The church has often fed people with empty spoons—giving them spiritual food without first finding out what their needs were, Clements says. "Now, through these programs, we feed them with a full spoon."

The church experiences some repercussions from people who are beginning to heal and to speak their minds. "That is something I think you need to prepare for," Clements points out. "I've heard an expression that I agree with: A sick person cannot live within a well household."

Divorce Support Group

Ruby, 59 and happily married for 35 years, teaches a Sunday School class for women aged 25 to 60.

Five years ago, the class realized a number of their members were divorced. One woman, who had been divorced by her minister husband, called Ruby often to talk. Finally, the woman said, "We need a support group where I can talk."

"You could lead it," the woman suggested. At the time, Ruby didn't know what a support group was. She asked her pastor's wife, who was working on a degree in psychology, to co-lead the group.

Ruby read books she could find on the subject. From her reading, she devised a list of guidelines for the group and distributed copies to members. The guidelines included rules concerning confidentiality and making "I" statements. "I didn't even know what an I statement was then, but I learned. Now we are firm about members not giving advice to others, but speaking for themselves only, unless a member asks for feedback," Ruby says.

The first two weeks, the only person who attended was the woman who had suggested the group. By the end of the month, five people were attending. It has continued to grow.

A church member, who was also a psychiatrist, taught the 8-week Southern Baptist Discipleship Training course, *WiseCounsel: Skills for Lay Counseling*. Through that course, Ruby learned additional skills for group leadership and for dealing with persons in crisis. She also completed a 50-hour lay counseling course offered in her community.

The divorce support group meets on Wednesday nights at the church following supper. The weekly topic evolves out of experiences of group members. "We usually open with asking, 'What's bothering you?'" Ruby says. "We deal with anger and grief a great deal."

Because Christmastime can be very stressful on persons, and many experience grief then, the pastor of the church preached a sermon on grief each January. He referenced the book *Good Grief* by Granger E. Westberg in his sermon. Ruby uses that book and a tape of that sermon to help persons when they first join the group. Ruby's co-facilitator is presently a man.

The group's format does not include formal prayer and Bible reading, but members address spiritual issues as they arise.

To Ruby's amazement, the group has lasted five years and shows no sign of ending.

"My Divorce Support Group Saved My Life"

Edna, a nonpracticing Mormon, started attending the divorce recovery group at Ruby's church when a church member who works with Edna invited her. "I was suicidal when I first entered the group. We meet on Wednesday nights, and by Monday of each week, I would be in bad shape.

"Three of us women in the group have been suicidal, and all of us state that if it had not been for the group, we would have killed ourselves. A man is currently suicidal. This group is literally saving lives."

Edna's divorce came about after her husband of 28 years announced suddenly that he would be leaving her to marry her best friend, with whom he had been having an affair. Edna had had a breast biopsy the day of his announcement, and her first response to her husband was, "I can't worry about that; I'm worried that I might have cancer." The test results turned out to be negative.

Then the divorce hit her. "When a person is hit out of the blue, she goes through a dysfunctional period when she doesn't know how she will get through the day." Edna had not admitted that her husband was an alcoholic. Her divorce attorney's first recommendation was that she start attending Al-Anon, an organization for family members of alcoholics, which she did.

Edna had allowed her husband to control her to the extent that when he left, she didn't even know what foods she liked to eat. She knew she didn't like the fried foods he had required her to cook for him, but she literally sat on the floor of the supermarket and cried the first time she went grocery shopping after he left. "I don't even know what I like to eat," she cried to her daughter. The daughter had to buy groceries for Edna for a while. Edna can now laugh and say, "That's the height of codependency."

Even though Edna attended church when she first married,

her husband, who had told her he would not go with her, gradually pressed her to stay home with him. "After he left, one of the hardest things I had to do was give myself permission to go to church. It felt so good to be back that I couldn't see through my tears."

Ruby, the support group leader, "doesn't talk about religion," says Edna. "But she talks about the fact that we are worthwhile people. This gives us a reason to keep going."

Edna knows two churches that operate divorce recovery groups for church members only. "This group invites anyone. Ruby knew I had been raised Mormon, but that didn't make any difference to her." Edna started attending the church until her job required her to work on Sundays.

The group follows an informal sponsorship plan. Ruby speaks privately to stronger members to keep in touch with those who need more help. The recipient of the care does not know about the "sponsorship."

Edna "sponsors" two suicidal women. She calls each one weekly. Typical activities include taking one on a Saturday night hayride and the other to a Sunday night concert. "I know what they are going through," she says with feeling.

Edna's daughter supported her mother emotionally throughout the divorce, especially since the former husband didn't speak to his daughter during the first year. Then, the daughter met with her father. After they met, "I felt hurt, angry, and betrayed," Edna says. "I blew up at my daughter." The two argued one night, trying to separate their angers. "I was carrying hers and she was carrying mine. I was angry at the way my ex-husband had treated her, and she was angry about the way he had treated me." After some hours, the two women sorted out their angers and agreed that each would carry her own only. "I see people coming into the group who are wanting to carry others' anger for them." Edna can be helpful in her responses since she knows about that process firsthand.

After nearly three years in the group, Edna considers herself recovered from the divorce experience. "Now I stay to pass on to others what I gained."

Support Group for Parents of Children with Special Education Needs

Briarlake Baptist Church, Decatur, Georgia, provides a support group for parents of children with special education needs. It meets twice a month while the children attend classes for them.

The parents started the group as a means to get together and talk about common experiences and problems. The format includes guest speakers and social activities for parents and children.

Briarlake offers four special education Sunday School departments and provides monthly Respite Care for parents. In the Respite Care program, Woman's Missionary Union members provide free child care from 10:00 A.M. until 12:00 P.M. on Saturdays to give parents a break. This service is open to the community, and the church has reached prospects through this ministry.

Support Group for Persons Separated, Divorcing, and Divorced

Robert Suggs, Minister to Singles at Second Ponce de Leon Baptist Church in Atlanta, offers six-week groups for persons separated, divorcing, and divorced. He found that it is best to offer a time-limited program. "It is hard to have an ongoing meeting since people work through their issues and leave," he says. "These people are transitional. They go through many emotional stages."

Suggs teaches the book *Beginning Again* by Terry Hershey to the groups, a book he calls "user-friendly." "Someone unfamiliar with church and Christianity can use it," he says.

The meetings take place from 4:00 P.M. to 6:00 P.M. on Sundays. Suggs found there is less competition for time then. About 15 to 30 persons attend each session.

During the first 30 minutes, a staff person who has experienced divorce lectures on dynamics involved in divorce. "A non-divorced person often gives advice and piety," Suggs comments.

For the remainder of the meeting, participants divide into small groups for confidential sharing. Participants stay in those same groups for the six weeks. Someone is designated to serve as facilitator in each small group.

In the program, leaders focus on the positive things God can do in one's life. "We teach that God's plan is one mate for life, but due to our fallenness, that doesn't always happen. God is forgiving and gives second, third, and fourth chances," Suggs explains. Participants are urged to make this a time of healing and spiritual renewal, during which their lives can be changed.

Suggs informs participants about the church's singles ministry, but some people travel as far as 35 miles for the six sessions, so becoming involved in church activities there is not always possible.

At the end of the six-week program, five additional classes are offered. These deal with practical situations encountered by divorced persons: the emotional impact of divorce; legal issues in divorce; finances for single parents; handling the ex-spouse, children, and family members; and re-entry into the job market. Experts within the church teach these classes.

Support Group for Single Parents

Kay Lynn Suttles, a single parent for eight years prior to remarriage, desired to start a single parent ministry at First Baptist Church, Atlanta. "Single parents feel so out of place in church," she says, "not married, yet not single."

The group started as a prayer group on Wednesday evenings. Over time, persons attending began staying afterwards to share concerns, and the group developed into a support group. Now participants stay two hours each week. Unwed mothers have begun attending.

The church offers a Sunday School class for single parents, and the parents opened a Swap Shop to share clothing and other items.

Addiction-related Support Groups

Understanding Addiction

Anyone who intends to provide a support group for persons recovering from an addiction needs to understand addictions.

In *The Addictive Personality*, chemical-dependency specialist Craig Nakken calls the process of addiction the steady, predictable development of an unhealthy "relationship with an object or event." Home missionary Edwin Lilly says, "Understanding that Christianity does not eliminate addiction in the lives of individuals and/or families, or that it in any way makes them immune to such an affliction, is a must for anyone who wants to be of help in ministering to alcoholics and drug addicts and members of their families.

"All too often many Christians tend to think that God provides an instant cure at the time of salvation. This is not so in all cases (probably the majority), and we must be willing to accept the fact that even Christians 'fall off the wagon,'" he adds.

People debate is alcoholism a disease or is it a sin. Usually, those who advocate the sin theory do so to blame the alcoholic and justify withholding help.

My friend Bill, a recovering alcoholic who received Christ some years after he had been in Alcoholics Anonymous, says, "I'm a sick sinner." When we recognize that one of the definitions of sin is "to miss the mark," surely turning control of one's life over to a chemical substance that causes severe problems in every important area of life causes a person to "miss the mark." It is a sin to be wept over.

Judgment blocks love and help. We can either judge or help. The question others must ask is, "What can we do to help?"

Spirituality is the first thing that goes when a person becomes addicted to a chemical substance. The same thing can happen for the family members because the family dynamics shift so that the family reacts to and takes care of the addict rather than takes care of its own agenda. As we help any addicted person recover, we are doing spiritual work.

Some Christians object to churches allowing nonsectarian groups (such as Alcoholics Anonymous) to meet in its buildings or to Christians attending such meetings. Lilly says, "The nonsectarian groups have done good work. They have done more than the churches have done, so why criticize them or why not work with them if we cannot provide something equal or better?" He advises, "There are enough hurting people whom churches are not helping. Let's support any group that helps people gain sobriety and freedom from drug addiction and that helps family members of addicts."

Lilly is a strong proponent of the use of church buildings more often, even if it means inviting nonsectarian groups to use the church.

What Is This Thing Called Codependency?

In my book, *Healing for Adult Children of Alcoholics*, I list one definition of codependency as "a dysfunctional pattern of living and problem solving which is nurtured by a set of rules within a family system. The rules are unwritten and unspoken but are powerful. It fosters exaggerated dependencies and interferes with our process of identifying our feelings. It is learned behavior that interferes with our forming relationships."

Codependency takes place within a family or societal setting where having feelings (especially negative ones) and expressing them directly are forbidden. Codependency can come from many sources: families with addictions to chemical substances, workaholism, gambling, sex, rigid religion; mental/emotional illness; and/or physical and sexual abuse.

Codependency is also an addiction to a person.

Persons addicted to codependency are spiritually empty, even though they may be very active in church activities. They can become addicted to religion, which becomes a religion of works. They feel guilty when they take care of themselves.

"Codependence," Walter Jackson writes in *Codependence and the Christian Faith* ". . . is an addiction: something to which you are compelled, something that once you begin it, you do not have the power to stop."[1]

How does codependency relate to the Christian life, since many biblical teachings, such as "serve others," seem to be codependent behavior?

Jackson declares that codependency is idolatry since we form an attachment with another person and serve others to find meaning for ourselves. "Nothing is to replace God," he says.

"Codependency as it is currently defined," says Jackson, "is certainly to be found in the church. If we look carefully, we will be able to see it there. It is my experience that when you learn the methods of codependence, even the most casual glance at most churches will reveal the presence of codependent behavior."[2] (My book *Shame on You!* has a lengthier treatment on the differences in codependency and Christian behavior.)

What is the way out of codependency?

Jackson say, "Spirituality is the place to begin to recover from codependency. And only a spiritual path will be able to deliver you from the ravages of alcoholism, chemical dependency, or codependency."[3]

Recovery from codependence calls for admitting that one is an addict, becoming involved in a 12-step program and working the steps, getting therapy from someone trained in this field, seeking a healthy church fellowship that does not operate by codependent rules or has enough flexibility for those rules to be challenged, and moving to the belief that one is accepted by God through the work that Jesus has done for us.

Support Group for Adult Children of Alcoholics

Terry grew up in a home with a violent alcoholic father. "When I turned 20, I recognized I had to do something," she remembers. "I started going to Al-Anon first. After a couple of years of working that program, I started dating Brad, who had gone through a recovery program. He had heard about Martinez Baptist Church, Martinez, Georgia, and about the support groups they offer, and he suggested that we come here.

"We started coming to church and to the Families Victorious meeting, and then the church started a group for Adult Children of Alcoholics. Every time I'd go [to it], it was such a blessing. I learned more and I heard healthy biblical messages. I learned how to put in healthy material [within myself] to replace all of the unhealthy that was put in when I grew up, not necessarily by my family, but by the world itself.

"I've learned to get in tune with myself and with God, and then I can get in tune with other people and relate to them better."

Many times, Terry felt as if she were the only person going through a difficult time. She felt all by herself in the world, and sometimes wondered if she were crazy. Now she knows that others in the group who grew up in alcoholic homes feel the same way she does, and that is a comforting feeling.

Brad had difficulty dealing with anger. Terry has learned to talk about feelings, so she will say to him, "You look like you're mad." The two will talk about what is causing the anger. Going to meetings has helped her to talk things out and to be more willing to open up, to get out all the misery that was crammed inside her.

One night at the meeting, the question was asked, "Growing up, what special friend did you have to talk to when things got bad?" Terry never had one, so from that point on, she prayed that God would send her that special friend.

"I didn't know that God would send me Brad, who became my husband."

The couple now uses the recovery tools they have learned in 12-step programs in their relationship. Their marriage has a better than average chance of surviving and of being healthy because of their willingness to work at having a healthy relationship.

Support Groups for Adult Children from Dysfunctional Families

Elaine Dooley has been a Church and Communities Ministry Consultant and Field Personnel Assistance Director for five years for the Western Baptist Association, New Mexico. She is employed by the Baptist Convention of New Mexico, and the position is funded by the Southern Baptist Home Mission Board. Formerly situated in Gallup, New Mexico, she now lives in Las Cruces.

For 12 years, Dooley worked with the Navajo Indians (six years as a volunteer and six as a paid employee) for the New Mexico convention's Language Department. Before that, she worked in California as a volunteer literacy worker with Mexicans.

Abandoned by a bivocational pastor-husband, Dooley is now divorced, and she uses that experience to minister to others who are separated and/or divorced. Using material developed by a pastor in New Mexico, Dooley offers weekend seminars and workshops. Those who attend these events then move into a support group. She calls the group Beginning Again Support Group.

She also uses the material to work with adults of divorced parents who never knew the absent parent and/or didn't have a relationship with that parent, and with adults who were victims of incest and sexual abuse from other sources.

The group tried using one Christian guide, but it didn't work. The guide pushed too hard to lead people to become Christians. Since the majority of persons who attend the group are non-Christians and non-Baptists, the approach drove them away. Now Dooley uses the 12 steps as written for Alcoholics Anonymous with the group. "The Plan of Salvation is presented in the first three steps," she says. In the group, Christian members speak freely and affirm their higher power is God.

For adults from dysfunctional families of all types, Dooley offers a 12-step program called Renewed Hope.

Support group meetings offered by Dooley last two hours, following this format:

1. Reading of the 12 steps
2. Serenity prayer
3. A reminder to respect the anonymity and confidentiality rule
4. Sharing time
5. Teaching time.

Dooley teaches the final half hour, encouraging dialogue among those present. Topics addressed include: What Is Alcoholism? Who Is an Alcoholic? Children Growing Up in a Dysfunctional Home, Adult Children, The Spiritual Life of the Adult Child, and Codependency. Completing the topics takes nine months; some people stay as long as two-and-a-half years in a group. "People in the Gallup area need much information regarding alcohol and drugs," Dooley says.

Using purchased Bible study material, the group looks at the Scriptures. "What do you want to look at in the Bible tonight?" Dooley will ask the group. A supply of Bibles stays in the room and members read them if they want. The person who reads a passage is invited to comment on what they've read.

Each meeting closes with a prayer, sometimes in Navajo, sometimes in Spanish, and sometimes in English. People hug before leaving.

No participant has ever walked out because of the biblical emphasis. One woman of another faith said at the first meeting she attended, "I didn't come for Bible study." She remained but sat through the session with her arms folded. The second meeting, she didn't accept a Bible offered to her. By the third meeting, however, she was peering onto her neighbor's Bible. The woman stayed in the group a long time.

"We're up front with what we do. We want people to know from the first meeting what they're getting into," Dooley says.

She conducted one Renewed Hope group in a native American church. "Native Americans are not in the denial that the Anglo/middle class people are," she observes. "They are more open, and it doesn't bother them if someone sees them go to a meeting." Since she has worked with Navajos for quite a while, some of the people know her. Dooley noticed that in the native American churches, the church leaders include children of alcoholics, recovering alcoholics, codependents, and parents of children abusing drugs. "Our leaders are bleeding to death of their wounds," she says. "We need to help them get healed so they will be able to lead the churches in healthy ways."

For years, white Americans said, "Navajos are nonconfrontational, and alcoholics must be confronted. The 12-step program

will not work with them." Dooley, however, has worked success-
fully with the native Americans. "The problems are the same,
and the solution is the same," she maintains. "When you confront in Christian love, they listen."

Helping High School Students Stay Sober

About 10 million American teenagers (more than half the
nation's junior and senior high school students) use alcohol weekly. More than 6 million teenagers, including some as young as 13,
have no problem obtaining alcohol.

Many "binge" drink to relieve stress and boredom. Of those
students who drink, 31 percent report drinking alone, 41 percent
said they drink when upset because it makes them feel better, and
25 percent said they drink to "get high."

Decreasing numbers of young people are using marijuana,
cocaine, and other illegal drugs, yet alcohol use remains high.
"They drink deliberately to change the way they feel," says United States Surgeon General Antonia Novello. "And we know that
the use of alcohol to, in effect, self-medicate is the trap door to
full-blown alcoholism."[4]

Many teens enter treatment facilities for alcohol and drug
dependency to bring about recovery. After leaving a program,
they then re-enter their local schools. Whether or not these students maintain sobriety depends a great deal upon the aftercare
program they follow. Pope High School in Marietta, Georgia, has
one of the best programs for students who are recovering addicts.

For recovering teenage addicts, starting back to school is
nearly as difficult as staying sober. Drugs have been their priority
for so long, they must change their thinking processes. Most
recovering addicts are older than their classmates because they
have failed classes and then have taken off more time for rehabilitation. Some say they have problems concentrating on school-
work.[5]

Peer pressure is one of the toughest things for these students
to deal with when they return to school—that and the reputation
for being "drug heads." Research shows recovering student-addicts
are offered some type of drug within the first 20 minutes after
returning to school from a treatment program.[6]

In addition, teachers must learn to adjust to changed students when the students return to school. The teachers are accustomed to these students being under the influence of drugs. The student-addicts must build a new image and surround themselves with new friends who don't drink or get high. For some, the most difficult part is breaking off relationships with people they really care about—and watching those old friends continue to get high.[7]

Two of the Pope High School counselors, Miriam Hanson and Debbie Peterson, have published a book on the subject, titled *How to Conduct a School Recovery Support Group*. Hanson responded enthusiastically to the question, "Could women in a church lead such a group in a local high school?" She suggested that an interested woman contact the counselor at her community's high school and offer to serve as co-leader with the counselor. "Laypeople feel inadequate and have a lot of fears about leading a group," she said. "They can actually do a very adequate job. They need to 'take the plunge,' and they will lose some of their fears." She believes that some counselors would welcome competent, caring assistance from people in the community.

An alternative would be to sponsor the group in a local church and notify schools of its existence.

Facilitators of such a group must become knowledgeable about alcohol and other drugs. Also, the adults must facilitate the group only and let the teens interact with their peers rather than the adults giving advice. Addicts handle each other best.

Support Groups for Persons Who Want to Quit Smoking

Fifty-five million Americans—nearly one-fifth of the population—smoke. Every year, almost half try to quit. Most do not succeed. Smoking-related diseases kill 390,000 persons annually.[8]

In *Smoker: Self-Portrait of a Nicotine Addict*, Ellen Walker writes, "I am an addict."

Her day-to-day functioning is dependent on using the drug nicotine. She doesn't function without it because everything about her past history with it says she can't. "If this personal relationship were with alcohol or cocaine," Walker states, "my symptoms would be different. I couldn't as easily pass myself off as 'normal.' My family would be more certain to know the fear and shame associated with living with an addict. I would likely have to resort to more extreme measures to finance and conceal my use. My remorse would be greater because of the more obvious emotional damage to my family and friends. But the person-to-person relationship—the heart of addiction—would be the same. It would be me and my drug getting through the day."[9]

"Drug dependency means just that," she continues. "We're dependent on something outside ourselves to give balance and meaning to our lives."[10] The drug becomes the center of the addict's existence, supplanting decision-making powers, often without the addict being aware of it. "The addiction becomes an additional member [of the family] and demands all the power, all the money, all the decisions."[11]

The souls of addicts don't show, Walker says. She believes that "it's nearly impossible for a nonaddict to know the self-deprecation, frustration, and fear of those who are held in the grip of nicotine."[12]

She poignantly states, "A kind of spiritual bankruptcy is a natural result of addiction, as a drug becomes the overwhelming power in our lives. It becomes a god of sorts. It never fails. It is always there. And it protects us from whatever we haven't wanted to deal with."[13]

Walker points out that because tobacco products have been accepted for so long as part of our culture, it's hard for us to think of users as addicts.

If a church wants to start a support group for smokers, it is best that a recovering smoker lead the group.

With this meeting, there would be no worry about smoking in the church building!

Weight Loss Support Group

Linda moved from California, where she had attended a Christian weight-loss support group, to Atlanta. "My weight started coming back when I was no longer working a program," she says. From material she had read, she knew the importance of staying in a group where one could be held accountable. "A friend got me into an Al-Anon group for relationship addictions."

"Food is my drug of choice," she admits. She talked with a couple of women about starting a weight-loss group. "For the first year, we flew by the seat of our pants, using *The Twelve Steps—A Spiritual Journey* and *Love Hunger*."

In the group, the women deal with issues such as the unhealthy behaviors of repression of negative feelings, enabling, compulsion, people pleasing, and caretaking as they relate to Christians. "Women, especially, are raised to please other people and deny themselves. The Bible teaches that we who know who we are in the Lord are to love the Lord first, and then to love self and others on an equal basis, beginning with ourselves," she says.

Everything that happens in the group is kept confidential. "Trust is one of our biggest problems, so we pair women who don't know each other to work on developing trust," Linda reports.

The group models healthy family life and a healthy Christian community. All the women attend church, but one woman says, "This is my church. At my church, I feel pressure to perform rather than feel accepted for who and what I am." Linda says that most Christians really do not believe that God accepts them as they are.

"Food addictions and workaholism are both approved in our churches," Linda maintains. Her father is a minister in a rigid denomination. "Church members may not use cocaine, but they still practice addictive behaviors."

The group meets weekly in her home for one-and-a-half hours. "Some women don't show weight loss as quickly as others, but they discover deeper issues—the root causes that lead them to overeat—that need resolution, healing, and forgiveness."

At first, women in her group wondered, "Why do Christians, who have salvation, keep falling back into unhealthy patterns and relationships?" They learned that many adults do not remember many of the abuses that happened to them. "We can't forgive until we know what happened," Linda emphasizes.

Linda emphasizes that the group is not into "parent-bashing," yet it provides a safe place for members to express anger toward parents for abuse. Eating helps women hide the unexpressed pain. Until they uncover the pain and express it in a safe place, they will keep on eating. All the diets in the world won't solve their problems—weight or otherwise.

Each woman uses the workbook *The Twelve Steps—A Spiritual Journey* and does homework suggested in it. This workbook serves as a guideline for the format of meetings. "Sometimes the work is so deep and so painful that we may stay on one step for two months. When we complete [the steps], we go through them again and again," Linda says. The group has structure, yet flexibility.

"The heart of the 12 steps is service," Linda points out. "In the church, we usually put the twelfth step first. Until Christians have done the first 11 steps, we're not ready to serve. When we have done those steps, the service will flow automatically."

[1]Walter C. Jackson. *Codependence and the Christian Faith.* (Nashville: Broadman, 1990) p. 48.
[2]Ibid, p. 136.
[3]Ibid, p. 114.
[4]"Junior high drinkers fight stress, boredom," *Marietta (Ga.) Daily Journal*, 7 June 1991.
[5]"Group helps students stay clean and sober," *Marietta (Ga.) Daily Journal*, 25 March 1991.
[6]Ibid.
[7]Ibid.
[8]Ellen Walker. *Smoker: Self-Portrait of a Nicotine Addict.* (San Francisco: Harper and Row, 1990) p. 14.
[9]Ibid, p. 60.
[10]Ibid, p. 66.
[11]Ibid, p. 72.
[12]Ibid, p. 6.
[13]Ibid, p. 108.

Grief-related Support Groups

The leader of a grief recovery support group needs to understand the dynamics of grief. It is not necessary for the person to have experienced a loss by death, although this would better equip her to understand members' experiences. If the leader has experienced such a loss, it should have occurred at least two years prior to leading a group, and she must have worked through her grief to a great extent before starting a group. The leader also needs to possess group leadership skills.

Grief follows an experience of loss. The appropriate feeling that accompanies grief is sadness. In *The Grief Recovery Handbook*, John James and Frank Cherry say that most of our problems come from unresolved grief issues in our lives.

In forming a grief support group, follow these steps.

1. Decide the focus. Will the group be geared to widows and widowers, persons who have lost other family members by death, or persons who have divorced?
2. Decide details such as meeting time and length (one-and-a-half hours once a week for 12 weeks is best).
3. Publish notices in all church publications, local newspapers, and cable television community bulletin boards. Alert local hospitals, funeral homes, counseling offices, and doctors' offices of the group's existence. In publicity, give specific and detailed information as to the group's purpose, meeting place, leadership, cost, membership, length of time for each meeting, and duration of group.

4. Locate a counselor, psychologist, or psychiatrist willing to lead a time-limited group (six to eight sessions) on a volunteer basis or for a small fee, or enlist a layperson to lead.

5. Set a limit for the duration of the first group. Future groups can be open ended.

6. Set basic principles:

- Grief recovery takes time.
- All feelings are to be expressed freely without judgment. No one will give advice, but instead will share out of first-person experiences and feelings.
- Members will focus on listening to others.
- Sharing needs to take place in the present rather than giving long monologues on past events.
- Confidentiality will be observed.
- Members are to make "I feel _____" statements rather than "You _____" statements to other members.

The five stages of grief include:

1. Shock: The person functions in a fog. He or she may feel numbness and think, "This isn't happening to me."

2. Denial: Some persons may deny the grief has occurred or that they feel pain.

3. Anger: The person may feel anger, especially at God.

4. Depression: The person feels immense sadness as the loss of the loved one sets in.

5. Acceptance: The person accepts the death and adjusts to life without the loved one.

Persons experiencing the death of a loved one will usually work through these five stages.

Bereavement Support Group

Jackie Deems suffered a triple loss: her child, who had multiple health problems, died; her husband couldn't handle the situation and left; and her grandfather died. Deems sought private counseling with David Walker, a minister in suburban Cleveland, Ohio, for 14 months.

After experiencing healing, Deems desired to help others who were experiencing the same trauma. Walker helped her research bereavement ministries in the greater Cleveland area, checking with hospitals and funeral homes especially. They found only a few such support groups, all provided by Catholic churches; none were sponsored by Southern Baptists.

Deems underwent an intensive nine-month Lay Counseling Training program through Moody Bible Institute. She then became Director of Bereavement Ministries for the Greater Cleveland Baptist Association. In this position, she is available to churches to speak about the grief process, how to comfort people, how to minister, and how to start grief support groups.

For four years, she tried to start such a group. Hospitals, however, told her she couldn't use the name of God in leading a group, and churches thought they were doing enough already.

People leave their churches because they are not being ministered to when there is a death, Deems found. Pastors and other Christians give platitudes to grievers, such as "just read your Bible and pray more, and all will be well."

Walker started a bereavement support group, GOAL (Going Onward After Loss), and Deems watched him lead it for two years. Then the Lord called her to lead the group.

"A group of peers is very helpful to grievers because they sometimes feel intimidated by professionally-led groups where the grievers think they are being analyzed," Deems notes.

"This ministry has taken over my life," Deems acknowledges. She has remarried and her husband, Bill, helps her. "If he were not as committed to our ministry as he is, I wouldn't be able to do it. He gives financial help as well as emotional support."

Walker tells Deems, "You're like a pastor to the people in the group. They call you on an anniversary date, you go to the funeral, and you call them afterward when no one else is around."

The first year of leading a group, Deems nearly went into a deep depression because she thought she had to make everyone feel better. She says, "Then the Lord said to me, 'You can't do that. Point them to me. Let them know that you survived, and they can, too.'"

"I Was a Member of a Bereavement Support Group"

Elaine, of Cleveland, Ohio, experienced a series of grief experiences. The first was the electrocution of her three-year-old son. For several months afterward, Elaine was in shock, and she thought she was going crazy. She became reclusive and stayed in her darkened house with the drapes drawn all summer, thinking of her son constantly. A bubbly person before, she stopped smiling.

She was already a Christian, but when she tried to read her Bible, the words were just words on paper. She says, "When I came into the support group GOAL, the Christians there let me know I was mad at God, and that was OK.

"I thought, 'If He loved me, how could He allow this?' He did allow it, and I felt angry. Through feeling and expressing anger, I was able to become reconciled with God. I don't know how or what I would do without Him." However, she finds that she does a very normal thing: she goes back and forth with the resolution of her anger.

Elaine's grief didn't stop with her son's death. In December 1988, she had a miscarriage. In March 1989, she had a tubal pregnancy, followed by surgery. In September 1989, she gave birth to a baby girl with spina bifida. The baby died.

Having been in the group, Elaine knew the process of grief better, but "knowing didn't help the pain. It was just as bad."

She comments, "In life, we don't have a class in grief, so we don't learn about it until we go through it. It's . . . important to have a Christian group to let us know it's OK to feel angry at God. That's what got me through to feeling better."

AIDS-related Support Groups

Acquired Immune Deficiency Syndrome (AIDS), the most dramatic disease to beset the human community in modern history, is also the most emotionally charged issue that Christians have dealt with in centuries. AIDS combines two of the most anxiety-ridden areas of human life: sexuality and death. More fear is generated by these two dimensions of life than any others. Fear causes people to react with hysteria and cruelty. Fear may even subject sufferers to greater suffering than they already have known.

The existence of AIDS calls for us to examine our deepest-held beliefs about how we value other human beings, how we minister to others, and how we judge others. Jim Pittman, pastor of the Valley Baptist Church in San Francisco, says, "In dealing with AIDS, Baptists are dealing with a multitude of issues that are tough for us, such as sexuality. Because a high percentage of PWAs (Persons with AIDS) are homosexuals, we draw back from loving them and ministering to them. Homosexuals need our love, our prayers, and our help."

What Is AIDS?

AIDS stands for Acquired Immune Deficiency Syndrome, an infectious disease that progressively destroys the body's immune system. A person with AIDS cannot fight infections and other diseases.

The disease was first identified in 1981. Since then, approximately 218,300 Americans have contracted AIDS. About half of these have died. There is no cure or vaccine for AIDS. Medical experts predict that by the end of 1993, 390,000 to 480,000 persons will have contracted AIDS, with 285,000 to 340,000 persons dying (cumulative from 1981).

What Causes AIDS?

The Human Immunodeficiency Virus (HIV) is believed to cause AIDS. The virus causes certain types of white blood cells to produce more AIDS viruses, which in turn attack healthy white blood cells. Since the white blood cells are vital to the body's immune system, they can no longer protect the body against illness. AIDS itself does not kill people; they die of other illnesses which their immune systems cannot fight off.

How Do People Get AIDS?

Most cases of AIDS are contracted from contact with infected blood or sexual contact with an infected person. Sixty-five percent of persons with AIDS are homosexual and bisexual males; 25 percent are intravenous drug users who share needles and other drug paraphernalia (including both heterosexuals and homosexuals); 4 percent are heterosexual men and women; 3 percent are adults and children exposed to contaminated blood through transfusions (before 1985, when all donated blood began to be tested for the AIDS virus); and 1 percent are babies born to mothers with AIDS. Heterosexual transmission accounts for an increasing proportion of AIDS cases.

The Centers for Disease Control reports that 1 million Americans, about 1 in 250, are infected with the HIV virus.

AIDS infection is growing most rapidly among women, minorities, youth, heterosexuals, and in the South. The statistics on college students with AIDS and prison inmates with AIDS are now equal.

More people have already died from AIDS in the last decade than died from the polio epidemic during a 40-year span. More people have died from AIDS than died in the Vietnam War. "It has become a major cause of death, and I don't see us having any serious decline in . . . mortality for the next decade," says a spokesman from the Centers for Disease Control.

The AIDS epidemic exists throughout the world. One hundred thousand women died of AIDS worldwide in 1990.

It is possible to be infected with the virus without developing AIDS, but it is still possible for that person to pass the virus to others.

What Is ARC?

AIDS-Related Complex (ARC) is a milder form of immunodeficiency than AIDS. In 1988, approximately 170,000 Americans were estimated to have some form of ARC and may develop AIDS.

At this writing, the diagnosis of AIDS is a death sentence. Eighty percent of those diagnosed will die within two years of diagnosis. The disease causes progressive weight loss, weakness, and disability. In its later stages, the person suffers memory loss and feels disoriented.

Some PWAs enjoy a prolonged time of strength and apparent good health.

AIDS can cause alienation and separation between the PWA and his or her support system. Some persons believe AIDS is God's punishment to persons with the disease.

Why care for or about a person with AIDS? One pastor responds by saying that Jesus died on the cross to bring God's unconditional love to all people without exception. Yet, the pastor acknowledges, it is true that AIDS bears a terrible social stigma. It has been called the new leprosy. In Jesus' day, many people considered leprosy to be a divine punishment for those afflicted, adding guilt to their physical suffering.

Jesus did not share these views about physical suffering or about the character of God. Jesus reached out and touched when persons with diseases dared to approach him. By so doing, He became ritually unclean, according to Leviticus 13. Jesus replied to criticism, "It is not those who are healthy who need a physician, but those who are sick" (Mark 2:17 NASB).

Jesus did not reject persons who were immoral; He presented God's compassion to them. The church today needs to respond in the same manner.

It is not up to us to judge why a person becomes sick; it is our task to view all persons as loved by God. At all stages of AIDS, patients and others in their lives need friendship and support.

Bill Lindsey, Southern Baptist chaplain at an Alabama state prison unit which houses prisoners with the HIV virus, says, "Persons with AIDS are precious people, too." He touches and hugs the men, explaining, "It's easy enough to tell a man you love him. You've got to show him." Lindsey holds hands while praying with a prisoner and tells him, "God gets no pleasure out of watching a man suffer."

Family members of PWAs suffer a similar stigma as the patient. Family members experience shock, anger, guilt, shame, and grief. They may be unable to tell others about the situation, which limits their support.

Persons who intend to lead AIDS support groups need up-to-date information about the disease; they need to know what PWAs and/or family members, loved ones, friends, and caregivers need; and they need to examine their attitudes toward PWAs. They also need a place to process their own grief as they deal with death and dying.

Before becoming involved in AIDS ministry, monitor your negative emotional responses (as registered by a tightness of the stomach, tensing of muscles, an intake of breath, feeling warm, feeling the need to put this book down, etc.) to the following situations. Gauge the strength of those responses on a scale of one to ten (ten being the strongest negative reaction).

1. A baby with AIDS born to a Christian mother who contracted the virus from a blood transfusion following surgery.
2. A baby with AIDS born to a crack-addicted prostitute of a different race.
3. A Christian woman who contracted AIDS through a blood transfusion.
4. A woman who contracted AIDS through sexual relations with her husband who led a worldly life-style before his conversion.
5. A man who contracted AIDS from his dentist.
6. A man who contracted AIDS through extramarital sexual activity.
7. A female who contracted AIDS through promiscuous bisexual relationships.

8. A young woman who contracted AIDS through premarital sexual relations with her fiance.
9. A heterosexual male who contracted AIDS from his wife, who contracted the virus from a blood transfusion.
10. A homosexual male who contracted AIDS through sexual relations.
11. A teenage girl who contracted AIDS through promiscuity.
12. A teenage girl, active in church, who contracted AIDS through a one-time sexual encounter.
13. A homosexual male with AIDS who came to Christ after learning of his disease.
14. A homosexual male with AIDS who went to his death unrepentant.
15. Your own heterosexual child who contracted AIDS.
16. Your own homosexual child who contracted AIDS.
17. A heterosexual sibling or parent who contracted AIDS.
18. A homosexual sibling or parent who contracted AIDS.
19. A hemophiliac who contracted AIDS through infected blood products.

Ask yourself the following questions:

1. Do I evaluate a person as being worthy of help on the basis of whether I view him or her as an "innocent" or "guilty" victim?
2. How would I want others to respond in attitude and actions if a member of my family or I contracted AIDS (regardless of how it was contracted)?
3. How do I believe Jesus would respond to all the examples listed above?
4. How do my responses match Jesus' responses?
5. On a scale of one to ten, how judgmental do I consider myself?
6. When I learn that a person has AIDS, do I think about or ask how the person got it? How important is that to my willingness to help the person?
7. How homophobic (have a fear of or aversion and hostility toward homosexuals and/or lesbians) am I?
8. Do I feel superior to persons with a different sexual orientation than mine?

9. When others speak in a judgmental way toward some of the situations listed above, do I speak up if I disagree or do I, by my silence, give consent?

10. Do I fear what others would think of me if I led a support group for PWAs or for their family members, loved ones, and friends?

11. To what extent do I justify my actions to critics rather than do what I think is right?

12. What degree of discomfort would I feel if I led a support group for PWAs or for their family members, loved ones, and friends? (Rate the comfort level for each group separately.)

13. To what extent might I feel critical of those who might take the position that my church should not provide a support group for PWAs or for their family members, loved ones, and friends?

14. To what extent am I concerned that my church present a caring presence in my community?

15. To what extent would I support my church providing support groups that might not lead to conversions? Groups that might lead to conversions?

16. To what extent would I be willing to lead a support group that would be enjoyable for me?

17. To what extent would I be willing to lead one that would be heavy, uncomfortable, and would drain me of emotional and spiritual energy?

18. If every church member had attitudes like mine, what would my church be like?

Support Groups for Persons with HIV, AIDS, and Their Caregivers

Darrell Ellsworth, bivocational pastor of Jewel Baptist Church in St. Louis, Missouri, was afraid of being called "the AIDS pastor," so he traveled 240 miles weekly for two years to help facilitate a group for PWAs. Each Tuesday evening, he and his wife drove the two hours to Columbia, Missouri, getting home at 11:00 P.M., exhausted.

"By 1983, I saw the AIDS epidemic coming, based on the statistics I was reading," Ellsworth says. "The grandson of a woman in my church died of complications from AIDS, and I went to the funeral home to visit the family. That brought the situation onto my doorstep."

Ellsworth began preaching that Christians need to follow the model of Christ—show compassion and look beyond the behavior to see a person for whom Christ died.

Then, Christians need to love and minister to the person. When he went to Columbia, he experienced homophobia—fear of, hostility toward, and aversion toward homosexual men and women. "I knew that [Christ] had died for them as surely as He did for me," he says. "When I developed an attitude that showed I was concerned, their appreciation helped [me] overcome my feelings."

After helping facilitate the group in Columbia for two years, Ellsworth lost his shyness about identifying with a ministry to PWAs. He learned of a young deaf man with AIDS, and Ellsworth attended group meetings with him to interpret through sign language. When the man moved, some in the group asked the minister, "Does this mean that you'll stop coming?" He stayed.

At one meeting, a man said, "I come from a Catholic background, and I was taught about a God of hate, vengeance, and punitiveness."

A second young man from a Protestant background spoke, "That was what I was taught, too."

A third man from another denomination echoed those sentiments.

Ellsworth, who had never spoken before in a meeting, could keep quiet no longer. "The God I know is a God of love, care, and compassion, and I've talked to Him today," he told the men.

A young man called Ellsworth a few days later. "I attended the meeting last week for the first time. The God you spoke of is not the one I was taught about. Could we meet?" The two visited for three hours. Now the young man attends church faithfully.

Ellsworth combined efforts with a neighboring pastor, Rick Lay of Harmony Baptist Church, to start a weekly support group for persons with the HIV virus.

Lay teaches a Bible study at each meeting, and the group closes with prayer. Ellsworth calls himself the bearer of medical information. He researches the latest material on available treatment.

Later, the pastors started a support group for family members and caregivers of PWAs. The two groups get together occasionally for a social outing.

Before he became involved in this ministry, Ellsworth says he "probably wouldn't have walked across the street to speak to a homosexual." But the people to whom he has ministered have made it worthwhile, he attests. He reports gratification on three levels: friendship with persons whom he would never have known; identification with fellow human beings—an observation of more similarities between heterosexual and homosexual people than he would have guessed; and seeing someone who has gone through trials related to faith and come through with either renewed dedication or conversion.

"When I see someone snatched from the jaws of eternal destruction and headed toward eternal life," he says through tears, "it's all worthwhile."

Ellsworth practices relationship evangelism. "We are not going to minister to homosexuals by pounding the pulpit and denouncing them," he asserts. "We must get to know them, care for them, and show them through our actions a God of love. Christ can redeem; I've seen it happen."

People sometimes ask Ellsworth, "Aren't you passively endorsing homosexuality by helping homosexuals who have AIDS?"

Ellsworth answers, "My adopted son is a drunk. My wife and I spent $34,000 on professional care to help him recover from his addiction. When I help him, I do not endorse alcoholism, I endorse him as a person."

One young man with AIDS, Ray, revealed to Ellsworth that he had received Christ as a teenager, but he believed his sins would send him to hell. Ellsworth had Ray recount his conversion experience and repeat John 3:16. The pastor then said, "God didn't give you everlasting life to take it away because you sinned." Ray returned to his home state to be with his mother and await his death. Ellsworth visited that home and conducted the funeral when Ray died seven months later.

"I have had a number of opportunities to give people from a faith background the assurance that their salvation was still secure—even Southern Baptists who had AIDS."

Some people ask, "Do these individuals have to be out of a homosexual life-style in order to come to your group?"

Ellsworth responds, "Absolutely not. We put our arms around them and love them into the arms of Jesus, if they don't already know Him." The majority, the pastor finds, come from a faith background but have been excluded by churches which didn't want to minister to homosexuals. "Many of these people are bowled over by a Baptist minister who concerns himself with persons with AIDS and with homosexuals."

Ellsworth has taught a four-hour workshop on AIDS ministry to churches and on university and high school campuses. A set of videotapes of that workshop is available for a small fee from the Task Force on AIDS of the Missouri Baptist Convention. See the resource list on page 93 for instructions on how to obtain the videotape set.

The following incident is typical of Ellsworth's ministry:

A Baptist pastor called Ellsworth a year after the seminar at his church to say, "My wife's brother is in the hospital dying of AIDS; would you visit him?"

The brother was a 23-year-old homosexual with only weeks to live. After talking a while, Ellsworth asked, "How do you feel about this sentence you've been given?"

"I'm ready physically and emotionally to die, but not spiritually," the young man answered.

"Would you like to get ready spiritually?" Ellsworth probed.

"Yes, but I feel like a hypocrite receiving Jesus on my deathbed," the man answered.

"Don't worry about that," Ellsworth reassured and began to read Bible passages to him. The young man listened receptively, but Ellsworth recognized after a period of time that he needed to leave.

He returned the next day, and the young man gave his life to the Lord. The two men wept together and rejoiced, praising God for His redemption.

"I Attend a Support Group for Family Members of PWAs"

Audrey's son, Bert, has AIDS, and his wife, Kathy, has the HIV virus.

The day before Bert's twenty-eighth birthday, his children called Audrey from a neighbor's phone. "Grandma, Mama says to come over right now because Daddy has cut the telephone wires."

"My husband and I rushed over," Audrey says. Bert lay in bed, having attempted suicide by taking an overdose of pills. He told his parents of his and his wife's horrifying situation. "I have AIDS, my wife has the HIV virus, and she is pregnant." Bert was still able to work then, but now he cannot.

Doctors wanted Kathy to have an abortion, but she refused. Since birth, the baby has been tested twice—negative both times—but doctors say antibodies from his mother may still be protecting him.

"I'm in mourning, I'm grieving," Audrey says, "and there are so few people I can talk to about this. I can't talk freely in church because people hide their heads in the sand and don't face real life. Ministers hide from the fact that we're in the midst of an epidemic that's going to affect all of us. I feel angry about that."

Audrey thought nobody knew what she was going through. Then a support group started at her church for family members and other caregivers of persons with HIV. She says, "[At this meeting] we can talk about what's going on and cry. We help each other. Because there is so much discrimination against persons with AIDS, it's a comfort to be able to talk with people who don't look down on my family because my son got AIDS. No one in the group thinks condemning thoughts against us or my son."

Audrey thinks some people blame parents for "raising a son who got AIDS." She sees people discriminating against the children of PWAs.

"When I see my son, I inhale him," Audrey says, "because I know I won't have him long."

Bert tried suicide a second time. He injected himself with an overdose of drugs and ran into the woods. Audrey and her husband searched for a long time, expecting at every turn to find Bert dead. When they couldn't find him, they returned home, and Bert walked into the house. His parents checked him into a hospital.

"I try to take it one day at a time, because the worst part is yet to come," Audrey says. "It's been hard up till now, but the hardest part is coming: the suffering that Bert will go through before he dies. It's difficult to see a child go first."

Rape and Incest Support Groups

Rape Crisis Support Group

Lora Smith, a divorced mother of three, has been a Mission Service Corps volunteer since 1985 at the Victory Baptist Chapel, Southern Baptist's only inner-city presence in Cleveland, Ohio, her hometown. Her official title is Director of Church and Community Ministries, but, she says, "Anything that happens between one Sunday morning and the next is my job."

Developing a rape crisis program at Victory Baptist evolved out of a number of avenues. Forty thousand people live in the square mile around Victory Chapel. One out of five adults cannot read; the unemployment rate is rising; and although the area is predominantly black, persons of 38 different ethnic groups live there. The population is changing: more women live there—both older women and younger women with children—who are divorced, have been abandoned, or have never married. Smith sees abused persons every day.

A key male leader in the chapel and his wife, Shirley (not her real name), were sexually abused as youths. Their daughter has been raped by boyfriends. Smith herself was a victim of sexual abuse.

Two years ago, she started teaching a series of associational workshops on social concerns, speaking on the needs of the elderly, as well as on problems such as housing, drugs, and alcohol. She brought in community leaders who were experts in the topics and invited a pastor to do a Bible study related to the topics.

One guest speaker came from the Rape Crisis Center. "We

need volunteers," he pled, so Smith signed up for a four-day Children's Assault-Prevention Program.

Shirley called Smith to help two sisters, young teenagers who had attended Victory Chapel. They were accusing their mother's boyfriend of sexually abusing them. Smith took temporary custody of the girls.

After six weeks, the girls left her home. Then other girls started reporting abuse.

Smith and Shirley underwent training offered by the Rape Crisis Center and manned the center's hot line for six months from 5:00 until 11:00 P.M. They became call-forwarding advocates to receive calls at all times. Now Smith also serves on the Center's speakers' bureau and is a hospital advocate for rape survivors. In June 1991, she started a Rape Survivors Support Group.

Smith's pastor, David O'Toole, is a bivocational minister. He holds a six degree black belt in the martial arts and owns a martial arts school near the church. Smith, his student, holds a second degree black belt and teaches Christian martial arts at O'Toole's school, as well as a weekly rape defense class at church.

"A lot of bad [things have] happened to me in my life," Smith says. "I believe God uses such situations for good."

Incest Survivors Support Group

Cheryl Fisher, 44 and married with a 17-year-old daughter, teaches kindergarten in her church, Noonday Baptist Church in Marietta, Georgia. Fisher has led an Incest Survivors Support Group at the church since 1989. She prefers that her real name be used in this book, along with the church's phone number— (404) 926-6138—so that women can call her if they need or want to.

"One Thanksgiving, our church held a special service, and I was asked to tell my story—which included sexual abuse from an uncle and physical abuse from my mother," she says.

"After that service, six women came up to me and said, 'Your story could be my story.' These were women who were singing in the choir and teaching Sunday School, women whom I would never have guessed had been abused, just as no one would have guessed it about me."

Her pastor urged her to begin a support group for such women. Her therapist told her, "You've had three years of therapy and you've been in two different [support] groups with me. You're qualified." Fisher decided to do it.

Before a person joins the group, Fisher interviews each applicant. Fisher lets her know what the group can do and what is expected of her, and she asks for a six-meeting commitment.

Fisher has found the hardest thing for her to do is to be patient, let the women struggle, and let them experience their own pain. Fisher gets supervision from three professional counselors, as needed. "Also," she states firmly, "I don't get out there without seeking God's help."

Fisher firmly believes that anyone desiring to lead this type of support group must be an incest survivor and must have undergone professional therapy. Fisher also considers it essential for a group leader to remember she is not a professional therapist (unless that happens to be her profession). "Remember what you are and what you're not. And what you are is good enough," she affirms.

A big part of the work of this group, Fisher has learned, is sharing among the women and educating them. "You don't make any judgmental statements to them," she says.

Fisher advises the women who participate in the group to find somebody outside the group with whom they can talk. "I don't want them to put all their eggs in one basket."

Fisher's satisfaction comes from seeing women who have suffered abuse work through their pain after going around it much of their lives. "They think the pain is never going to end and that it's going to be so overwhelming and so scary. But seeing other people who have worked through it gives them hope."

Support Groups for Families of Prisoners

Bill Goins, of Tucker, Georgia, does what he knows best: he works with prisoners and their families. Goins is a retired Baptist pastor, a retired prison chaplain, and retired Director of Chaplains for the state of Georgia. He and his wife, Maxine, lead a support group in their home for families of prisoners. Statistics reveal that many prisoners and their wives suffered abuse as children and become abusers as adults. In ministering to these persons, Goins follows Jesus' words in John 21:15, "Feed my lambs" (KJV). Goins serves as a right arm to churches. "I share the basic things of the faith with these people," he states. "I treat them with respect and stand with them during this difficult time."

"Families 'do time' just as the prisoners do," Goins maintains. One event that horrifies him is churches sometimes drop families of prisoners once the person (usually a male) enters prison. Some family members have actually had a committee or an individual in the church say to them, "We prefer that you go somewhere else."

"This goes against all the principles of the gospel," Goins asserts.

"The local community thinks that once the prisoner goes away, he is gone forever," Goins observes. In reality, "nearly 100 percent return to their homes, except for those who are executed or who die in prison. The community must, at some time, be faced with the ex-prisoner becoming integrated into the community. The church needs to maintain contact with the family . . . during the incarceration period and after the prisoner returns."

"Church members don't know how to handle prisoners and their families, so churches avoid those people. Judgmental attitudes are also at work when this happens," Goins believes. He helps spouses find churches who will accept them in spite of their "stigma."

Goins helped one couple, exiled from their church during the man's imprisonment, find a new church after the man's release. "I feel very good about that type of incident," Goins says. "I care as much about the ninety-and-nine as I do the one lost, and that couple would have been lost to church life as things were going. I think we need to be concerned about conserving those who are already saved." He tells these couples to find a church because they need what it has to offer.

Goins also serves as pastor of a nonexistent church—the wives, husbands, mothers, fathers, boyfriends, and girlfriends of prisoners. They are black, white, Jewish, Catholic, Protestant, male, female, rich, poor. "I started out working with 'nobodies,' but now I have people from every level of society: a woman from the corporate setting whose son got into drugs, a schoolteacher whose son is in prison. And, it's amazing how well they fit together in the support group." Goins says, "Some of these women have been the best pastors and therapists to each other." The women call one another throughout the week and minister to each other. Goins pairs a newcomer in the group with someone who has been involved a while.

Group members also confront one another. The girlfriend of a man who killed his wife and stabbed a son and daughter was brought up short by the other members of the group. "What makes you think he's going to love you?" The girlfriend broke off the relationship.

Most male prisoners write their wives, "You're too young and pretty to wait for me. Go ahead and get a divorce. I won't feel bad." Actually, the man fears his wife will leave him, so he takes the initiative to protect himself. When the wife gets the letter, she feels rejected and angry. Group members help her interpret what he means. However, Goins has found it's hard to help the men whose wives do leave.

Group members call Goins when they experience trouble.

They invite him to important family events. He and his wife also attend trials, which means a lot to the families. "Don't get into this work if you don't want lots of phone calls," he warns.

Group members gather at the Goins' home for a New Year's Eve party. Holidays are especially lonely times for families of prisoners, so group members try to get together at those times. They have Christmas dinners, summer picnics, and other events. "They are lovely people to work with once they know you care," Goins has found. "Sometimes adult children can't forgive [a parent] for being a criminal and they alienate themselves from the [parent], and the [other parent] travels a lonely road."

Group members send birthday cards to prisoners and have birthday parties in honor of the prisoners. When a prisoner is released, the group celebrates.

Goins' primary task is to keep hope alive for families while helping them face reality. "Families react and want a quick fix; mainly, they want to get the prisoner back home," he comments. He does some "pretty heavy" counseling for those who want a "bandage" to get through the night.

One of the most gratifying things Goins does is to conduct marriage enrichment seminars for male prisoners and their wives—in the prison setting. "These marriages are under more stress than any other, therefore, they need more help. I'm keeping hope alive for these folks." For the seminar, wives come in for the day. Each seminar pushes a tough schedule—from 8:00 A.M. to 4:00 P.M. As few as 4 couples and as many as 22 have attended. Goins covers such topics as communication, intimacy, and conflict resolution.

Goins focuses on how couples will handle the first year of adjustment after prison. "This is like the first year of marriage," he points out. "If the couple doesn't handle this effectively, the marriage will not survive."

After a prisoner is released, he or she needs counseling and may be required to get it. Goins contacts these former prisoners because their spouses have attended the group. Goins knows the situation and may have had private sessions with the spouse.

Goins has performed some marriages between former male inmates and girlfriends, and some couples repeat their vows in a local church after the prisoners' return. The group gives showers to such couples.

Families of prisoners experience the same dynamics as in a death. The difference is, in a death, a person can wrap up the experience, resolve the grief, and go on with life. When a family member goes to prison, he or she is still alive. The five stages of grief include:

1. "I can't believe this is happening to me." The person experiences shock, disbelief, and denial.
2. When reality dawns, it is so painful that the person can hardly stand it.
3. When the person adjusts to the pain, anger sets in. One woman "cursed like a sailor" and railed at Goins. "Where were you when I needed you? I beat a chair to pieces in my living room when I realized what my husband had done."
4. The person adjusts to circumstances which may be painful. One pastor's wife moved out of a large parsonage in an affluent community to an economy apartment, a traumatic experience for her. "For the first time in my life," she said, "instead of looking at inmates and families of one of them, I'm one of them."
5. The person accepts the reality of the situation.

"The remaining spouse must learn who she is and how to get her needs met under the circumstances," Goins says. "Her social needs change—she can no longer associate with her husband's friends. Her physical needs are [still] there. Some women sleep with many men to ease their loneliness. They must develop a system of friendship to get them through. They usually have a big economic adjustment. The average family barely makes it with two incomes, and when the man's income is taken away, the family can be destitute. Sometimes the wife travels many miles to visit her husband and the old car breaks down on the way."

For a wife, the primary concerns after her husband has been sentenced include: Where will he be assigned? What will be his routine? How often can the family visit him? Where will the visits take place? What will be his work detail?

Some prisons have industries, while others have high school

74

and college educational programs. "Prisons try to match needs with abilities," Goins says, "but sometimes the priority is determined by an empty bed." Prisons try not to put inmates near their homes.

Persons who want to work with the families of prisoners need to understand the penal system. Goins recommends that volunteers become acquainted with their local and state prison systems. A chaplain or other official can give a tour of the facilities.

Sometimes a prisoner will complain to the family that he is not receiving adequate medical treatment. The family will become anxious and angry. However, prisons cannot afford to neglect an inmate's health for fear of lawsuit, so such stories need not be believed. The inmate often has better medical care than family members.

Goins also recommends that volunteers visit the diagnostic center of a state or federal prison system and observe as much of the entry process of a prisoner as allowed. "This process, while necessary, dehumanizes a person," Goins says. For a male inmate, "his hair is clipped short, he is stripped, and disinfectant is poured over him . . . , and the uniform given him probably doesn't fit." Goins found the process depressing to watch.

Next, the inmate undergoes a complete medical checkup. He is checked for disabilities and undergoes a mental health examination and social history to decide what type of security he needs and which institution suits him best.

The prisoner's family is "on hold" during this time. "They know nothing," Goins says. "The inmate sometimes stays in the county jail six months."

During the first month after the prisoner is placed in a prison, the family cannot visit. This rule is intended to help prisoners accept the reality of prison. The family, however, wonders about his safety, his medical needs, and so forth.

Perhaps the most essential thing for a volunteer to remember is that she must not take the responsibility for fixing everything. "One woman in my group has a son in a prison in another state, sentenced to 25 years for killing his ex-wife's boyfriend. I can't get that son out," Goins says.

Services that could be provided for families of prisoners

include taking a family member to the doctor, picking up food from a food pantry, picking up needed medicine, taking a family to visit the prisoner, picking up a sick child at school, helping prepare for a wedding or funeral, or taking the family to church or school functions.

The cardinal rule in dealing with this population is to never give anyone money. "Prisoners are great con artists," Goins comments. "Many times a wife or mother sends her last cent to the man who gambles or buys cigarettes."

Inmates will do thoughtful acts in jail that they would never have done outside, Goins notices, such as send cards on special occasions. Churches could give batches of all-occasion cards to prison chaplains for use by inmates.

Dunwoody Baptist Church, Dunwoody, Georgia, makes their bus available to take family members to visit inmates. Volunteers take refreshments for the trip and help with needs along the way. "You may change a diaper or hold a sleeping baby," Goins smiles. "You may see inner-city children marveling over seeing the first cow of their lives. One four-year-old boy saw his father for the first time."

Volunteers especially should not claim that they know what the relative of a prisoner is going through (unless she has gone through that particular experience). A volunteer can ask the family member, "What can you tell me to help me understand what you are going through?" Listening respectfully is a valuable contribution to a family member.

"Evangelism is 'caught' in this work rather than taught," Goins says. "As I deal with these people, I share my faith and pray. Sooner or later, these people are going to find some things that are bigger than they are. Although I don't teach the Bible at meetings, I always bring out some Bible teaching in my comments. At the close of each meeting, we hold hands and pray. They respect me as a minister and they listen." Nearly 100 percent of those he deals with are church members. "We're not dealing with a lost population," he finds.

"This work is a heartwarming experience," Goins adds. "This is not a miracle thing, but when people hang in there and work through things, that must be a miracle."

He concludes by saying, "Some people do come to know the Lord through this type of ministry, but if that's all you're going in there for, you're going to miss the main point—ministering to hurting people in Jesus' name."

Goins makes his address and phone number available for readers who would like to contact him regarding possible training for volunteers: 516 Jordan Drive, Tucker, Georgia 30084, (404) 921-7839.

"My Husband Went to Prison"

"Was the shame the worst thing you felt?" I asked Martha, a weary, gray-haired, 58-year-old woman who must have been very pretty in younger years. Her husband served a two-and-a-half-year sentence for crimes related to a gambling addiction.

"It was just pain," she said, her eyes filling with tears. "The shame was there, too, but when I drove three hours each way to visit him once a month, it was primarily pain that I felt."

Martha, a nurse and mother of ten children, never considered herself an independent person. "Even with my husband's income, we barely made ends meet. So when he went to prison, I felt so scared. And I still do," she added.

Tom, her husband, is now home on a monitor program. This means he has the same restrictions as in prison but is living at home. He must notify the police about his moves, and he is required to attend meetings of Gamblers Anonymous.

The two youngest children, both girls, were in high school when Tom went to prison. They both dropped out of school. They resented Martha's asking them to pay rent, so she took on a second job to meet financial obligations. "That tired me out so much, I had to quit the second job," she said. The youngest girl moved in with her boyfriend.

Soon after Tom left, Martha came down with a staph infection and stayed in the hospital for three months. The family had no medical insurance. Someone referred Martha to the Department of Family and Children's Services, which paid the enormous bill. She had to pay the doctors' fees. A garnishment was put on her wages.

"That [experience] was one of the scariest times," she remembers. "I called my church to talk to the pastor. He was not in, but the secretary sent me to a lawyer-friend of hers who helped me work it out with the other lawyer. I still pay some each month."

Martha attended a few meetings of Gam Anon, an organization for spouses of addicted gamblers. "Those women [at Gam Anon] said I was the most in denial of anyone they had ever known," she said with an apologetic laugh. "They asked me if Tom had taken a second mortgage on our house without my knowledge, which they said was common [of husbands who gamble]. I insisted that he hadn't. Sure enough, when I checked, he had." She lost the house and had to find another place to live.

She didn't care for the advice-giving style of the other women in that Gam Anon chapter, so at the suggestion of her son, a counselor, she joined Codependents Anonymous, a support group for persons who are codependent. She attends weekly meetings and finds them helpful. At one point, Martha, a member of another denomination, heard of a support group forming at a Baptist church for families of prisoners. It never came into being. "That would have helped me so much," Martha emphasizes. "No one can imagine what a terrible experience this is [being married to someone in prison] unless she has been there. I felt as if I were going under."

She started crying again. "I still feel so scared. Tom had to obtain a job before he could get out, but it's selling on commission, so the income is uncertain." Tom thinks he can persuade the two younger girls to return to high school. "I hope he has more luck with them than I do," she said, wearily.

"Can anybody understand how scared I feel?"

Support Groups for Women Who Have Had Abortions

Julie, a Christian and a nurse, learned of an emotional disorder called postabortion syndrome (PAS) experienced by many postabortive women. Undergoing an abortion can cause devastating emotional aftereffects. Concerned, Julie asked her church to sponsor a support group for women who have had an abortion.

"For some women, sharing within the support group is the first time they have shared openly about their abortions," Julie reports.

The support group facilitators stress anonymity. Members should not talk about other members outside the group. Members exchange names and phone numbers and contact one another during the week.

"Several guidelines make our meetings more productive," Julie says. The group opens with prayer, asking God for transparency with one another so that the sharing will be open and honest. "Another important guideline is to listen to others without interrupting." A final guideline involves commitment to the group meetings. Some members must arrange child care and drive long distances to attend the meetings.

Each women is asked to set goals for her recovery, such as: "I will tell my husband about the abortion I had before I met him"; "I will forgive my mother for encouraging me to abort"; "I will forgive myself for having the abortion." A goal which all members embrace is, "I will strive to be the woman God created me to be, not the woman into which my past has molded me."

The group is based on Christian principles, but "it would be foolish to think PAS is just a Christian problem," Julie says. "It can affect any woman, regardless of her religious background."

It is preferable that the group facilitator also have experienced abortion. Greater rapport might then be established between group members and the leader. If that is not possible, the facilitator must have experienced a serious grief in her life. Before facilitating a support group, the woman must have worked through either experience and resolved her grief. She needs to understand the dynamics of grief in general.

The facilitator needs to be knowledgeable about fetal development, the abortion experience, and postabortion syndrome. She also needs to be in touch with her own position regarding abortion.

"I Suffered from Postabortion Syndrome"

Twenty-five years ago, Diane, 18-years-old and ignorant about sex, became pregnant. Her family disowned her.

She stayed in a home for unwed mothers until her baby was born, then she gave up her daughter for adoption. For the next three years, she lived a self-destructive life-style.

She became pregnant again twice but did not tell either father. Abortion was illegal then, but Diane obtained one both times. Something went wrong with the second abortion, and doctors feared she might die of blood poisoning.

Several years ago, Diane became a Christian, and this change filled a great void in her life. But inside, Diane knew something still wasn't right.

A few years ago she visited a Christian counselor who knew how to help her discover the root of her problems. "It was wonderful to grieve for the first time," she says. "I had to accept the responsibility for the abortions and learn to forgive myself."

"God has granted me the ability to grieve without shame. Now I am . . . helping other women overcome the pain and grief of their own abortions by co-leading a support group for other women who have had abortions."[1]

[1]Human Development Resource Council, Inc., "Life Support," Spring/Summer 1991. (Norcross, Georgia). Used by permission.

Churches with Support Groups

Kingsland Baptist Church

Timothy Sledge, child of an alcoholic father, pastors Kingsland Baptist Church, Katy, Texas, near Houston. "One of our goals is to be a healing place for hurting people without regard for whether or not the persons we help become a member of the church," he says.

After coming to terms with his own past, Sledge preached a series of sermons in 1988 on adult children of alcoholics. When the series began, he sent out a notice for the start of a support group for adult children of alcoholics. He thought he would get enough response to start two groups; enough persons showed up for six groups. A staff member with some background in recovery work led two, a laywoman trained in counseling led one, and Sledge led two. He called the groups Face-to-Face Groups. The church now has a counselor on staff who leads support group meetings.

Since then, the church has expanded its ministry to hurting persons. On Sunday afternoons, the church provides a walk-in open meeting for persons interested in recovery issues. A recovery Sunday School department is provided using study materials geared to persons in recovery. Quarterly, on a Sunday night, the church features Recovery Night. All support group participants are invited, and Sledge's sermon topic relates to recovery. At the end of the service, support group leaders stand at the front and people come forward to pray. Rather than making a general statement such as, "I want to live a better life," persons respond to the sermon topic and say something such as, "I want to deal better with a certain authority figure in my life."

The church is tremendously pleased with the support group ministry. "Groups are very powerful, positive experiences, where people make significant changes in their lives," Sledge says.

In his studies on small groups, Sledge concluded that a 12-meeting format works best for family of origin issues. Members commit in writing to miss no more than three meetings. "The attendance is nearly perfect," Sledge says, "because needs are being met." The church has provided 30 support groups in two-and-a-half years.

After the initial support groups ended, Sledge wondered if there were more people who needed this program. New people appeared. "We recognized this situation is not like a glass of water that we will drain dry. The number of people who need this help is endless."

The church mails out publicity on groups, but a large number of the participants learn about them by word-of-mouth. Many persons come from other churches or have no church affiliation.

Each participant pays a $50 fee plus $51 for tapes and a note-book. "We have experienced no resentment whatsoever about the fee charged," Sledge reports. "I'm sure that part of that comes from the fact that we turn no one away. If someone does not have the money, we find a way to help."

Sledge notes that the meeting time and place are important considerations. "We started having meetings on Wednesday nights, but occasionally a child would pop into the room or children would be giggling outside in the hall. If someone is crying in the group about some pain, the place needs to be private and secluded. We now meet on quieter nights of the week in more remote parts of the building. On a practical note, we buy large quantities of tissues. It's important to have comfortable chairs. People who are new to the church need to know how to get to the room. We use a registration process during which the person learns how to find the meeting place.

"Outlining expectations to the member is important. We ask—but do not force—individuals to refrain from use of any mind-altering drug—legal or illegal—(including alcohol) during the 12-week period. We ask individuals taking mood altering prescription drugs to check with their doctors to see if they can discontinue the medication during the group process. We ask single persons to refrain from sexual activity during that period. All of those involvements can be used by people to avoid getting in touch with their feelings."

Participants use a simple phrase, 'I support you,' when a person is having a hard time emotionally during a meeting. Maybe he is crying or having a hard time sharing some material. Another member can spontaneously say, 'I support you.' It's sort of like saying, 'Amen.' It helps the speaker very much."

Sledge built the Face-to-Face meetings on a technique called "checking in." It includes: What are you feeling right now? What issues are you dealing with? What has happened to you since our last meeting?

Sledge notes that the strength of the group process lies primarily in the fact that when one person starts sharing his experience, listeners think, "That sounds like my story; I'm not alone in the world."

"Bonding takes place between members and they support each other. Some things are easier to talk about in a group. For example, a woman might feel uncomfortable talking to the pastor about something in a private session, but she might feel more comfortable talking about it to a number of people. It might seem to be the opposite, but actually the larger number provides a protection and the speaker feels less inhibited because of the trust that develops in the group," he says.

In 1991, the church started Heart-to-Heart groups which deal with the present, changing one's behavior now. Sledge developed material for them similar to other 12-step programs. Titled "Cycles of Recovery," its activities help members move through the 12 steps within group meetings.

What is the impact of these various groups on the church?

"We have many people who have gone through the recovery program. They don't wear badges, but their lives have been changed and they have moved into different facets of church life. Some people [who participate] come from other churches in the community and then go back to participate in their own churches in a different dimension. I am happy when our work makes contributions to other churches—it's all God's work.

"We put no pressure on group members to join our church, but research shows that the more times a person visits a church prior to joining, the more likely he is to stay in the church after joining. The Southern Baptist mentality has been, 'A person walks into the church and we must see him walk down the aisle the first day he is here.' Research indicates that type of convert is not likely to remain connected to the church. Each visit to the church deepens the bond the person has to the church." Kingsland's baptisms average more than 100 per year.

"We are currently involved in starting home Bible studies which are outreach oriented and where people study the Bible in a supportive atmosphere but without an emphasis on recovery from dysfunctional families," Sledge adds.

Sledge has written *Making Peace with Your Past*, a guide for developing support groups for adult children from dysfunctional families. It is part of LIFE support group ministries developed by Discipleship Training. See Suggested Reading on page 90 for more information.

Roswell Street Baptist Church

It's hard to believe that someone with such a lanky body (6 foot, 5 inches), contains such a big heart. If you'll pardon the pun, it's also hard to believe that someone with his head in the clouds has such a down-to-earth approach to ministering to hurting people.

Nelson Price began pastoring Roswell Street Baptist Church, Marietta, Georgia, in 1965. Today, the church has 8,000 members and is one of the largest Southern Baptist congregations in the Southeastern United States.

Price explains his philosophy of ministry in this way: "Jesus is the only Door, but the church must provide as many doors as possible to bring people to the Lord."

Roswell Street's varied ministries exemplify this philosophy. For example, some years ago, Price led the church to open a Crisis Pregnancy Center to provide an alternative to abortion. Since then, more than 2,000 babies have been born who would have otherwise been aborted.

Then the need arose for a home for unwed mothers, so the church bought a beautiful Southern mansion that accommodates six young women at a time.

In January 1989, Price led the church, which he describes as a congregation of especially compassionate people, to develop a recovery program for alcoholics and drug addicts. Rapha, a Christian hospital for alcohol, drug, and psychiatric treatment, used Roswell Street as the site for a pilot program to train laypersons to facilitate Christian 12-step programs.

Church leaders examined the congregation for individuals who had had an addiction and had been through a rehabilitation program. They asked these individuals if they would be willing to complete 13 weeks of intensive training on how to lead a group of persons struggling to overcome some addiction. Rapha provided the training for those persons who were willing. It consisted of 13 weeks of lectures and in-service training in groups. These individuals then became facilitators of support groups for persons struggling with some addiction.

Then Price saw a need for codependency support groups. "In a Bible-centered, conservative church, 24 out of 36 women stated an interest in such a group. The problems are right here in our churches," he states emphatically.

All of these ministries, Price says, are based on compassion. "We believe we should accept people as they are but help them to become all that God desires for them to be."

Suggestions for Other Growth Groups and Support Groups

Changing jobs
Facing unemployment
Facing retirement
Dealing with long term illness—Alzheimer's Disease, cancer, etc.
Survivors of suicide attempts
Stroke survivors
Spouses of stroke survivors
Battered women or men
Survivors of rape
Stepfamilies
Stepparents
Dealing with difficult children and/or teenagers
Arthritis and other health-related issues
Young widows and/or widowers
Marriage enrichment
Newly married
New parents
Mothers of preschoolers
Homemakers
Persons experiencing Premenstrual Syndrome

Works Cited

Books

Clinebell, Howard. *Growth Groups*. Nashville: Abingdon, 1978. *

Jackson, Walter. *Codependence and the Christian Faith*. Nashville: Broadman Press, 1990.

Nouwen, Henri J. *The Wounded Healer: Ministry in Contemporary Society*. New York: Doubleday, 1979.

Right Step Christian Recovery Program Facilitator Training Manual. Houston: Rapha Publishing, 1990.

Walker, Ellen. *Smoker: Self-Portrait of a Nicotine Addict*. San Francisco: Harper and Row, 1990.

Unpublished Manuscripts

Platt, David. "A Program of Spiritual Group Support for Pastors in the Greater Boston Baptist Association," Dmin. diss., Southern Baptist Theological Seminary, 1989.

Shirley, Charles. "The Religious Discussion-Interaction Group:

An Experience in Small Group Ministry." Dmin. diss., Southeastern Baptist Theological Seminary, 1973.

Suggested Reading

Deits, Bob. *Life After Loss*. Tucson, AZ: Fisher Books, 1988.

Diedrich, Richard C. and H. Allan Dye. *Group Procedures:Purposes, Processes, and Outcomes*. Boston: Houghton Mifflin Company, 1972. *

Drakeford, John W. and Claude V. King. *WiseCounsel: Skills for Lay Counseling*. Nashville: Convention Press, 1988.

First Place: A Christ-Centered Health Program. LifeWay Press, 1992.

James, John and Frank Cherry. *The Grief Recovery Handbook: A Step-by-Step Program for Moving Beyond Loss*. New York: Harper-Collins, 1989.

Hanson, Miriam and Debbie Peterson. *How to Conduct a School-Recovery Support Group*. Marietta, GA: Hanson Associates, 1991.

The Health Consequences of Smoking: Nicotine Addiction. Rockville, MD: U.S. Department of Health and Human Services, 1988.

Johnson, David W. and Frank P. Johnson. *Joining Together: Group Theory and Skills*. Englewood Cliffs, NJ: Prentice-Hall, Inc., 1975. *

Levy, Steven J. *Managing the Drugs in Your Life: A Personal and Family Guide to the Responsible Use of Drugs, Alcohol, and Medicine.* New York: McGraw-Hill Book Co., 1984. *

Martin, Sara Hines. "AIDS Comes to Church," *Church Administration*, Nashville: Sunday School Board, SBC, 1991.

Martin, Sara Hines. *Healing for Adult Children of Alcoholics.* Nashville: Broadman Press, 1988.

Martin, Sara Hines. *Shame On You! Help for Adults from Alcoholic and Other Shame-Bound Families.* Nashville: Broadman Press, 1990.

Nakken, Craig. *The Addictive Personality.* Center City, MN: Hazeldon Educational Materials, 1988.

Oates, Wayne E. *Pastoral Care and Counseling in Grief and Separation.* Philadelphia: Augsburg Fortress, 1976.

Search for Significance LIFE Support Edition. Nashville: LifeWay Press, 1992.

Smith, Harold Ivan. *I Wish Someone Understood My Divorce: A Practical Cope Book.* Minneapolis: Augsburg Fortress, 1986.

Smoke, Jim. *Living Beyond Divorce: Working Guide.* Eugene, OR: Harvest House Publisher, 1985.

Sledge, Timothy. *Making Peace with Your Past* Leader's Guide. Nashville: LifeWay Press, 1992.

Sledge, Timothy. *Making Peace with Your Past* Member's Book. Nashville: LifeWay Press, 1992.

The Twelve Steps for Christians. San Diego: Recovery Publications, 1988.

Woititz, Janet G. *Guidelines for Support Groups*. Pompano Beach, FL: Health Communications, Inc., 1986.

Asterisk (*) indicates books out of print. Please contact your library for copies.

Resources

AIDS National Hotline: 1-800-342-2437

Alcoholics Anonymous World Services, Inc., General Service Office, 475 Riverside Drive, New York, New York 10115. (212) 870-3400.

Booth, Sylvia, Home Mission Board, SBC, 1350 Spring Street, NW, Atlanta, Georgia 30367-5601. (404) 898-7000.
Booth assists churches in starting crisis pregnancy centers.

Fisher, Cheryl, Noonday Baptist Church, 4121 Canton Road, NE, Marietta, Georgia 30066. (404) 926-6138.
Fisher works with an incest survivors support group.

Focus on the Family, 801 Corporate Center Drive, Pomona, California 91768.
This organization produces material for a New Hope for Adult Children of Alcoholics group.

Fresh Start Seminars, Inc., 63 Chestnut Road, Paoli, Pennsylvania 19301. (215) 644-6464.
This organization provides seminars in churches and other settings for the separating, divorcing, and divorced individual.

Goins, Bill, 516 Jordan Drive, Tucker, Georgia 30084. (404) 921-7839.

Goins works with prisoners and their families in adjusting to life while in the prison system and after being released. Contact Goins if you desire more information on sponsoring support groups for families of prisoners.

Human Development Resource Council, Inc., 3961 Holcomb Bridge Road, Suite 200, Norcross, Georgia 30092. (404) 447-0759.

Through the use of scientifically accurate materials and visually dynamic audiovisual presentations, the Human Development Resource Council, Inc. (HDRC), a nationally recognized non-profit educational organization, increases public awareness of the amazing development and humanity of the preborn child and related topics such as abortion, teen pregnancy, and sexually transmitted diseases.

Giant Step Productions, P. O. Box 471, Barker, Texas 77413.

Giant Step Productions produced the following cassette tapes of sermons by Tim Sledge to aid support groups in staying on course.

"The Gift of Freedom for Adult Children of Alcoholics." 12 messages, $29.95.

"Codependency: Taking Care of Yourself." 4 messages, $13.95.

"Attitudes, Actions, Change." 15 messages, $34.95.

"Making Peace with Your Past" audiocassette. Nashville: LifeWay Press, 1992.

Missouri Baptist Convention, Missions Department, 400 East High Street, Jefferson City, Missouri 65101. (314) 635-7931.

Missouri Baptist Convention has produced "AIDS Ministry Video," a set of four videos on ministry to persons with AIDS. $20.00 for set, plus $1.25 for postage.

Nicotine Anonymous World Services, 2118 Greenwich Street, San Francisco, California 94123. (415) 922-8575.

Overcomers Outreach, Inc., 2290 W. Whittier Boulevard, Suite A-D, La Habra, California 90631. (310) 697-3994.

Overcomers Outreach is a ministry to chemically-dependent/compulsive people and their families through Christ-centered 12-step support groups. These groups are not intended to replace the traditional programs of Alcoholics Anonymous, Al-Anon, etc., but are designed to be a supplement from the Christian perspective.

Putnam, Ann, Home Mission Board, SBC, 1350 Spring Street, NW, Atlanta, Georgia 30367-5601. (404) 898-7000.

Putnam assists churches in developing support groups for persons with disabilities.

Rainbows for All God's Children, Inc., 1111 Tower Road, Schaumburg, Illinois 60173. (708) 310-1880.

Rainbows is an organization that provides support groups for children who have suffered any severe loss such as from death, divorce, etc. Training and materials are available.

Serendipity House, P. O. Box 1012, Littleton, Colorado 80160. (303) 798-1313.

Serendipity House is a Christian publisher of materials for support groups with a Bible study format.

Stephen Ministries, 8016 Dale Avenue, St. Louis, Missouri 63117. (314) 645-5511.

This organization, used by 62 denominations, trains pastors and laypersons for Christian caregiving and lay counseling.

Sara Hines Martin, a counselor in private practice in Marietta and Acworth, Georgia, specializes in working with adult children of alcoholics and persons from other shame-bound families. She also teaches seminars internationally on the topics of adult children of alcoholics and shame-bound families. She is also an adult child of an alcoholic.

Martin received her education at Carson-Newman College (B.A.), Southwestern Baptist Theological Seminary (M.R.E.), and Georgia State University (M.S.). She has done additional study at the School of Pastoral Care, North Carolina Baptist Hospital, Winston-Salem, North Carolina.

Martin has also written *Healing for Adult Children of Alcoholics* and *Shame on You! Help for Adults from Alcoholic and Other Shame-Bound Families*.